Meaningful First Communion Liturgies

The Complete Planning Guide for Catechists and Teachers

Nick Wagner

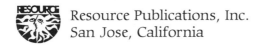
Resource Publications, Inc.
San Jose, California

Also available in the CELEBRATING THE SACRAMENTS series:
Eucharist! by Susan S. Jorgensen
Children's Catechumenate by Philip J. McBrien

Reprint Department
Resource Publications, Inc.
160 E. Virginia Street #290
San Jose, CA 95112-5876
(408) 286-8505 voice
(408) 287-8748 fax

Library of Congress Cataloging in Publication Data
Wagner, Nick, 1957-
    Meaningful first communion liturgies : the complete planning
guide for catechists and teachers / Nick Wagner.
        p.   cm.
    ISBN 0-89390-432-5 (pbk.)
    1. First communion. 2. Catholic Church—Liturgy. I. Title.
    BX2237.W34   1998
    264'.0203—dc21   97-52019

Printed in the United States of America.
02 01 00 99 98 | 5 4 3 2 1

Editorial director: Nick Wagner
Music consultant: Peggy Lovrien
Production: Mike Sagara, Elizabeth J. Asborno, David Dunlap

Cover photograph: W.P. Wittman Limited, Toronto, Ontario
Author photograph: Perry Chow

If, then, you wish to understand the Body of Christ, listen to the apostle as he says to the faithful, "You are the Body of Christ, and his members" (1 Corinthians 12:27). If, therefore, you are the Body of Christ and his members, your mystery has been placed on the Lord's table, you receive your mystery. You reply "Amen" to that which you are, and by replying you consent. For you hear "The Body of Christ," and you reply "Amen." Be a member of the Body of Christ so that your "Amen" may be true.

—St. Augustine (Sermon 272)

Contents

Introduction

If you are a typical director of religious education, school principal, teacher, or catechist, you are too busy to read this book. But don't worry. You don't have to read it all at once. If you were hoping to find a "just add water" outline of the liturgy that you could use next month or next week, there are a couple in Appendix C. But I hope you won't stop there.

The principles in this book are meant to be integrated, over time, into the general parish process for initiating candidates into first communion. However, this is not a catechism nor preparation program for first communion. This book is only about the first communion liturgy itself.

But it cannot be "only" about that liturgy because any liturgy of the church is integrated into not only all the other liturgies of the church but also into all the other ministries of the church and all the members of the church. By its nature, liturgy touches and transforms everything.

So while this book is "only" about the first communion liturgy, it is also about much more. It is about how the entire parish initiates candidates into the eucharistic banquet. It is about how the liturgical life of the parish shapes these candidates. It is about all the work and prayer that goes into preparing this important celebration in our communities.

The book is divided into the four parts of the Mass and each of the elements within those parts is discussed along the following outline:

◆ Purpose

◆ Planning comments

◆ Role of the assembly

◆ Role of the first communicants

◆ Preparation for the following groups:

  ◆ Pastoral planning team (including the catechist)

  ◆ Parish

  ◆ First communion families

  ◆ First communion candidates

The reader can deal with all of the elements of the liturgy or only with those that she or he thinks require the most attention in a given parish. Within each element, the reader might choose to deal with all the aspects discussed in the above outline or only with those concerning the first communicant.

At the end of each major section of the book are Catechist Background Sheets. Some of these are designed to be supplementary material to help catechists understand some element of liturgy that is related to the first communion celebration; others are helpful tips to make the first communion liturgy run more smoothly and effectively. You can photocopy and hand the sheets out to catechists for their own information, or you can use them as a basis for discussion at a catechist training session.

Another way to take advantage of this book is to use it as supplementary material to your current first communion preparation program. Appendix A outlines some of the more popular programs. I have indicated which parts of this book could possibly be integrated into the various stages of those programs.

This designed method of picking and choosing illustrates an important bias of mine: Nothing is carved in stone. I have made my case for the direction I have set out in this book. It is up to the reader to weigh my reasoning, take what works, and adapt the rest. There is only one principle that can never be violated if we are to remain true to the mandate of the Second Vatican Council. In the celebration of the liturgy, the full, conscious, and active participation of the assembly is the aim to be considered before all else.

This leads to another bias of mine. The primary place for anyone to be *involved* in liturgy is as a member of the worshiping assembly. Often we attempt to make some group feel involved in the liturgy by giving them a role in the sanctuary. The other side of that logic is that when this group was singing and praying with the rest of us, they (and we) were not involved. It is a subtle but real division of the faithful to extract some of our members for liturgical service solely so "they" will be involved. I recognize that often we do *not* feel involved when we worship. But the solution to that is to upgrade our worship, not to divide the body.

What that means for the reader of this book is that I am advocating that the first and best place of involvement for the first communion candidates is as worshiping members of the assembly. Calling on these candidates to serve the assembly in liturgical ministries—even if they might be qualified—not only divides the assembly; it also seems inhospitable to ask someone we are initiating into full communion to minister to us when our clear call is to minister to them.

My final biases have more to do with definitions. In this book, I use the word "catechist" almost exclusively. I use that word in the sense it is used in the *Rite of Christian Initiation of Adults* to mean the person or persons (other than the parents) whose primary task it is to communicate and transmit the faith to these candidates. That could be the DRE, the principal, a teacher, a classroom catechist, or a parish volunteer.

I also refer to "first communion" instead of "first Eucharist." That is because first communion candidates have celebrated many

Eucharists. The fact that they have not yet been able to share communion does not mean they are anticipating celebrating Eucharist for the first time.

And I usually refer to the person who is the object of preparation as a "candidate" instead of a "child." This is first of all to reinforce the understanding of the first communion celebration as a step in the initiation process. In the Rite of Christian Initiation, the catechumens are referred to as "candidates for initiation." I also use "candidates" because not everyone preparing for this celebration is a child. However, the overall thrust of the book does assume that the reader is dealing primarily with young children.

Preparing to Celebrate First Communion

When a catechist, liturgist, or planning team prepares to celebrate first communion, there are a few basic things to keep in mind: when to have the celebration, how to make the celebration special, and how to make sure the celebration is liturgically good.

When to Have First Communion

Season: When candidates celebrate their first communion, they are celebrating the culmination of their initiation into God's family. From this moment on, they will be full and active participants in the liturgy. That means they will also be participating in the celebration of the liturgical year. Through the guidance and example of their family and catechists, they will grow in an understanding of the spirituality of the liturgical seasons and their importance in the life of Catholics.

First communion candidates, therefore, should learn that there is a season for initiation, a season for first communion. That season, of course, is the Easter season. There is no requirement that first communion *must* be celebrated in the Easter season. In fact, there may be good reasons why some first communions are celebrated at other times of the year. But the catechist will want to help shape the spirituality of the candidates in such a way that the candidates understand Easter as the season of initiation and as the premier time for celebrating the initiation sacraments.

Day: Just as initiation has a season, it also has a day. The day for initiation is Sunday, the day of resurrection. Again, this is not a requirement. It is an emphasis. It is a way of shaping the spirituality of the young people who will be preparing for this important event. Many larger parishes schedule several times for first communion on the weekends in Easter. Because of the numbers of candidates, it is sometimes necessary to have first communion on a Saturday. However, this can always be thought of as an exception to the ideal.

Time: The time of day for first communion is not so important. If the number of communicants is small, planners may want to consider scheduling first communions during the regular Sunday liturgies. However, when the number of first communion families begins to fill up more than a few rows of pews, that might be a cue to consider Sunday afternoons as an option. (Again, larger parishes may have to schedule them during regular Masses *and* in the afternoon.) What is important is that the liturgy be well celebrated with strong musical leadership, good presiding and preaching, and full and active participation by the assembly.

How to Make the Celebration Special

It is right and good that the planners and families strive to make the experience of first communion a memorable one. However, sometimes we can lose sight of what is really important.

The most important aspect about first communion is—*communion*. That seems obvious, doesn't it? But how often have you noticed families or other planners focusing on what the candidates will wear, what they will carry up during the preparation of gifts, what special decorations will be in the church, what songs the candidates might sing, etc., while nobody pays attention to the bread and wine? The meal gets ignored.

At their first communion, the candidates are, for the first time, carrying out Jesus' mandate to "do this in memory of me." The "this"—the thing we do to remember Jesus—is sharing a meal. To make the candidates' action of remembering Jesus special, it is most important that planners and families focus all their energy on making the experience a meal.

That, of course, means eating real bread and sharing from the cup. At this point, you can probably hear the excuses starting to be raised about why that just isn't practical in your parish. I can promise you that if you go to a larger (smaller), richer (poorer), more liberal (more conservative) parish, excuses will always exist about why communion does not look and feel like a meal.

It comes down to this. We can either say it is impractical to do what Jesus asked us to do, or we can do what Jesus asked us to do. Jesus asked us to break bread and share the cup—to have a banquet in memory of him. That is the most special thing we can do.

Basic Principles for Celebrating The First Communion Liturgy

Even if you are not the primary planner for the first communion liturgy, you will need to know three basic principles about the liturgy in order to prepare the candidates. Understanding these principles is not difficult. You probably already know them. The difficulty comes in consistently and carefully applying the principles in actual planning.

First Principle: Active Participation of the Assembly

The most basic principle in the liturgy is that it is the work of the people. It is not the presider's job or the musician's job or your job to make the liturgy work. It is the work of the people. The job of the parish leaders is to do everything possible to facilitate the work of the people. Parish leaders must make the liturgy accessible to the people so they can participate in a fully conscious way.

Adding or changing parts of the liturgy makes it more difficult for people to participate. This is a little bit counter-intuitive. Our instinct tells us to add a special song or change the ritual a bit or do something different with first communion so people will wake up and participate more. Unfortunately, this usually has the opposite effect. When things are "different," especially in church, people tend to get out of sorts. They wind up resisting the very changes you hoped would inspire them.

That does not mean *nothing* can be changed. But in planning, always remember the basic principle: The liturgy is the work of the people. Let them do their job by keeping things as familiar as possible.

Second Principle: Word and Eucharist

The next basic principle is that the liturgy is a two-part celebration of word and Eucharist. These are not two separate elements that happen to be thrown side by side. They work together to help us know who God is and to strengthen us for our mission.

In the Liturgy of the Word, we are called by God to do the work of the Gospel. All the readings and the homily work together to help us learn who God is. But the readings and the homily should not be thought of as "teaching" in a classroom sense. It is more the sense of lovers "learning" about each other as they spend time together. The words are important, but what is behind the words is much more important.

If we truly hear God's word, we cannot help but be stirred by it. The stirring up of our hearts makes us want to respond. Our response is the Eucharist. Called to faith by God's word, we put our faith into action by doing what Jesus asked us to do. We remember him through the sacred banquet.

Catechists will want to spend a great deal of time and energy helping the first communicants see the structure of word and Eucharist in the Mass and helping them understand its importance. If catechists are helping to plan the first communion liturgy, they will want to work hard to make sure these two elements are the most important things in the Mass and that they are not obscured by smaller, less important elements of the liturgy.

Third Principle: Eucharist Leads to Action

Every Eucharist commissions us to carry out the mission Jesus left us. We are sent forth from Mass to build the kingdom of God's mercy and justice.

It is important to remember each of these principles when planning any liturgy but especially when planning the first communion liturgy. If you are ever in doubt about the appropriateness of an action, an omission, an addition, or any element of the liturgy, scrutinize it against these three principles.

Conclusion

First communion can be a pageant or it can be a celebration of God's grace in the life of the parish community. The way the liturgy is planned and celebrated will determine which of these happens in your parish the next time first communion is celebrated. By paying attention to when the liturgy is celebrated, paying attention to the meal itself, and paying attention to good liturgical principles, you can be assured that your community will have a grace-full liturgy.

May God's face always shine upon you as you take on this very important task for your community.

Abbreviations of Documents Cited

CSL	Constitution on the Sacred Liturgy (*Sacrosanctum Concilium*), Vatican Council II
DMC	Directory for Masses with Children
EACW	Environment and Art in Catholic Worship
FIYH	Fulfilled in Your Hearing: The Homily in the Sunday Assembly
GILH	General Instruction on the Liturgy of the Hours
GIRM	General Instruction of the Roman Missal
LMIn	Lectionary for Mass: Introduction, second *editio typica* (1981)
LMT	Liturgical Music Today
MCW	Music in Catholic Worship
RBC	Rite of Baptism for Children
RCIA	Rite of Christian Initiation of Adults

PART ONE

Opening Rites

Opening Rites

Overview

The opening rites are a collection of songs, prayers, and actions with a single goal: to ready the assembly to hear the word of God. The two most important parts of the opening rites are the opening song and the opening prayer. The opening rites contain so many elements that it can be difficult to keep the focus on preparing the assembly to hear God's word. Take care not to *add* to the opening rites with lengthy announcements and ritual directions.

Outline of the Rites

Bracketed text indicates optional rite.

◆ [Gathering]

◆ Opening Song

◆ Sign of the Cross and Greeting

◆ [Introduction]

◆ Rite of Blessing and Sprinkling with Holy Water

    (or)

◆ Penitential Rite

   ◆ Invitation

   ◆ Confiteor

    (or)

   ◆ Kyrie

◆ Gloria (not done in Advent or Lent)

◆ Opening Prayer

Catechist Background Sheets

◆ Opening Song

◆ Penitential Rite and Sprinkling Rite

◆ Opening Prayer

Recommended Reading

Johnson, Lawrence J. "Immediate Preparation and Introductory Rites." *The Word and Eucharist Handbook*. Rev. ed. San Jose: Resource Publications, Inc., 1993. 2ff.

People in love make signs of love, not only to express their love but also to deepen it. Love never expressed dies. Christians' love for Christ and for one another and Christians' faith in Christ and in one another must be expressed in the signs and symbols of celebration or they will die (MCW 4).

"Introductory Rites." *The Mystery of Faith*. Washington, DC: Federal Diocesan Liturgical Commission, 1981. 125–134.

Jungmann, Josef A. "The Opening or Entrance Rite." *The Mass of the Roman Rite: Its Origins and Development*. 2 vols. Translated by Francis A. Brunner. New York: Benziger Brothers, Inc., 1951. Reprint (2 vols. in 1), revised and abridged by Charles K. Riepe, *The Mass of the Roman Rite*, Westminster, Md.: Christian Classics, Inc., 1978. Restored to 2 vols., 1986. 261–390.

Wagner, Nick. "How should the priest greet the assembly on Sunday?" and "What are the introductory rites?" *Modern Liturgy Answers the 101 Most-Asked Questions about Liturgy*. San Jose: Resource Publications, Inc., 1996. 25–27.

Planning for a convergence of pathways to the liturgical space in a concourse or foyer or other place adequate for gathering before or after liturgies is recommended. In some climates this might be outdoors. Such a gathering space can encourage introductions, conversations, the sharing of refreshments after a liturgy, the building of the kind of community sense and feeling recognized now to be a prerequisite of good celebration (EACW 54).

Gathering

Purpose

The coming together of the community is not listed as an official part of the opening rites. Nevertheless, it is essential to have a gathering of people in order to have liturgy. The gathering begins almost as soon as people leave their houses. Driving into the parking lot, coming into the church, and finding a seat are all part of the gathering. If the gathering is done well, if people are hospitable to one another as they enter, if the atmosphere is comfortable, the liturgy will be off to a good start.

The first communion liturgy usually throws everyone just a little off balance, making a relaxed, hospitable atmosphere difficult. Work extra hard to keep things running smoothly as people come together.

Planning Comments

One of the easiest ways to help everyone feel more comfortable and welcome is to make sure everything is ready well before they arrive. Get the microphones in place and tested. Turn the lights on. Pick up any clutter both inside and outside. Make sure the musicians complete all their warm-ups. All this needs to be set at least thirty to forty-five minutes before Mass begins. If your Masses are spaced tightly, you will need to become efficient at setting up quickly.

Also, have greeters at all the entrances; sometimes "side" entrances are left unattended. Ask the greeters to be especially alert to the candidates' guests who are not parishioners.

If the musicians are up to it, plan some prelude music that begins about twenty minutes before Mass. This can be choir solos or instrumental music or both. Here are a few suggestions for prelude music.

◆ "Sheep May Safely Graze," J.S. Bach

◆ "Solemn Processional" from the *Water Music Suite in F Major*, George Frederick Handel

◆ "Trumpet Tune in D Major," Henry Purcell

◆ "Prelude in C," J.S. Bach

◆ "He Shall Feed His Flock," George Frederick Handel

Role of the Assembly

It is important that the assembly not think of themselves as guests in the church. This is *their* home. Each member of the assembly needs to be hospitable and welcoming just as we are in our homes. The members of the assembly will want to especially extend themselves to the candidates and their families as they arrive.

Role of the First Communion Candidates

The role of the candidates is to arrive early. The reason for this is *not* so the planning team will not have to worry so much—although that is a useful side effect. The reason is so the candidates can have plenty of time to relax and greet each other and put themselves in the proper mood for worship. Hurried, last-minute entrances are not conducive to worship.

Preparation

Pastoral planning team

The catechist can best prepare for this moment by getting everything done ahead of time that can possibly be done. In life, there are those who can delegate and those who can't. If you can, give away every single task on your list so you can focus on the gathering with the candidates and their families. If you are not a delegator, start early, very early, getting all the little set-up jobs out of the way so you can be mentally and emotionally present to the families at least forty-five minutes before the liturgy begins.

The rest of the pastoral team will also want to be ready well ahead. The musicians can welcome the gathering assembly with prelude music. The presider can be out front greeting people as they enter. Members of the liturgy committee and catechetical committee can be on hand to greet and to help out with last-minute details.

The parts preceding the liturgy of the word, namely, the entrance, greeting, penitential rite, *Kyrie, Gloria*, and opening prayer or collect, have the character of beginning, introduction, and preparation.

The purpose of these rites is that the faithful coming together take on the form of a community and prepare themselves to listen to God's word and celebrate the eucharist properly (GIRM 24).

Parish

The parish can prepare for this moment by assuring there is an adequate and hospitable place for gathering. All new and renovated churches are, of course, constructed with a gathering space. In older churches, space might be made available by removing a few of the back pews. At the very least, all the entryways should be kept spotless and made to look as inviting as possible.

First communion families

First communion families can prepare for this part of the liturgy throughout the preparation process by arriving at church early enough to be able to meet and chat with other parishioners. It can be difficult getting the family to church soon enough to do this, but it can be done with some effort. By getting to know other members of the community, the first communicant will feel more a part of the parish and more a full member at the table.

On the night before the celebration itself, families can prepare by getting all the clothes, car keys, sunglasses, purses, and other details ready so getting ready in the morning will go quickly and smoothly.

First communion candidates

Church can often feel boring and burdensome to younger people. Part of the candidate's preparation can be to practice *beginning* the liturgy with a good attitude. Again, getting to church on time for the gathering in order to meet and get to know more people will help.

Opening Song

Purpose

 The purpose of the opening song is to join together as a community in a single action.

We come into the church as individuals, but then we join together in one voice and one heart to begin our worship. God speaks to us as a community of believers, so it is important that we perform this communal act in order to *hear* God as a community of believers. It is our first action together.

Of these parts the entrance song and the opening prayer are primary. All else is secondary (MCW 44).

The two processional chants—the entrance song and the communion song—are very important for creating and sustaining an awareness of community (MCW 60).

The entrance song should create an atmosphere of celebration. It helps put the assembly in the proper frame of mind for listening to the Word of God. It helps people to become conscious of themselves as a worshiping community. The choice of texts for the entrance song should not conflict with these purposes (MCW 61).

Planning Comments

Because the opening song is so crucial to our worship, it must be a song everyone knows and sings well. It does not have to be focused on the readings or even on first communion. But it must be a song that will actively engage the full participation of the assembly.

The opening songs that work best are those with a strong beat because they accompany a procession. The opening song should *feel* like we should march to it. The opening song also works best when the assembly knows it by heart.

- "Gather Us In," Marty Haugen
- "Bring Forth the Kingdom," Marty Haugen
- "All Creatures of Our God and King"
- "Alleluia, Sing to Jesus"
- "Morning Has Broken"

Role of the Assembly

The role of the assembly is to give full voice to the opening song. It is not a matter of singing along with the choir. By each individual adding his or her voice to the song, each person is contributing to the work of the community. To not sing is to refuse to help with the task at hand. By contributing as fully as possible to the work of the community, the members of the assembly are providing a strong role model for the first communion candidates.

Role of the First Communion Candidates

The role of the candidates is to participate as members of the assembly, following the examples of their elders in faith. They also will want to focus on allowing the Spirit of God to work through them as the community becomes one in the singing by the power of that same Spirit.

Preparation

Pastoral planning team

The catechist can best prepare for this part of the liturgy by understanding the crucial nature of the opening song. It is very easy at a "big" liturgy to get distracted by things like the order of the procession, the logistics of seating, the photography arrangements, etc., leaving the "usual" things like singing to take care of themselves. Yet the well-prepared catechist will remember that the primary and overriding principle of the liturgical reform is the full, conscious, and active participation of the assembly. The first moment this participation becomes necessary is in the

After the people have assembled, the entrance song begins as the priest and the ministers come in. The purpose of this song is to open the celebration, intensify the unity of the gathered people, lead their thoughts to the mystery of the season or feast, and accompany the procession of priest and ministers (GIRM 25).

singing of the opening song. Archbishop Annibale Bugnini, one of the key architects of the reform, wrote, "Profound participation in such a celebration is inconceivable apart from its joyous expression in song. The Constitution [on the Sacred Liturgy] regards singing as 'a necessary or integral part of the solemn liturgy' (112)" (*The Reform of the Liturgy 1948–1975*, trans. Matthew J. O'Connell [Collegeville, Minn.: The Liturgical Press, 1990], 47).

The pastoral planning team can best prepare for the opening song by assuring that the parish has adequate musical leadership and resources to make the opening song a worthy one that will join the community together. The musicians in particular will want to keep the number of opening songs limited until the parish has mastered them and sings them well.

Parish

The parish can prepare for this moment by learning at least a few strong opening songs by heart over the course of the preparation time for the first communion candidates. In that way, they will be able to fully participate from the very beginning of the first communion liturgy.

First communion families

First communion families prepare by being role models to the candidates, singing robustly during the ordinary Sunday Masses and other liturgies that lead up to the first communion liturgy.

First communion candidates

Candidates prepare by learning about the importance of the opening song and, along with the parish community, learning some opening songs by heart. The more the candidates can practice the opening song that will be used for the first communion liturgy, the less nervous they will feel.

Opening Procession

Purpose

The opening procession is one of the best examples of the "inefficiency" of the liturgy. Generally, we see the presider, cross bearer, candle bearers, and lectors go *from* the altar area *to* the front entrance of the church (before the liturgy "starts") only to make a more formal, reverse trip a few moments later.

The purpose of the procession is obviously not to get the ministers into their places. It is instead intended to say something about who we are as a worshiping community. The members of the procession are part of us. As part of us, they are symbolizing that we are a dynamic community, a community on the move, a community that is not satisfied with the status quo. We

A procession should move from one place to another with some purpose (not simply around the same space), and should normally include the congregation …. The design of the space and arrangement of the seating should allow for this sort of movement. There should be concern for the quality, the gracefulness, and the surety of this movement. Seating arrangements which prohibit the freedom of action to take place are inappropriate (EACW 59).

follow the Lord's command to pick up our cross and follow. The procession symbolizes this commitment.

Planning Comments

The members of the procession would include at least the presider and one of the lectors. The procession would normally also include a cross bearer and candle bearers. On special occasions, it might also include an incense bearer. The first communion liturgy would be a fitting occasion to use incense.

Role of the Assembly

The role of the assembly is to participate in the procession either by actually walking in it or by watching it as it goes by. If they need to have their heads in books, being part of the procession is difficult. If the assembly does not know any processional songs by heart, a strong refrain-verse song is a good choice. The assembly can then at least sing the refrain without using their books.

Role of the First Communion Candidates

The candidates might be part of the opening procession for the first communion liturgy. However, if the candidates are going to be in the procession, it would be appropriate to also include their families. The role of the family would then be highlighted in the opening procession.

Preparation

Pastoral planning team

The pastoral planning team can help prepare for this procession by assuring that all the members of the procession are well rehearsed. This is particularly important if the procession for the first communion liturgy is different in some way from the usual Sunday procession.

Parish

The parish as a whole has no particular preparation for this moment.

First communion families

First communion families will prepare for the procession by being available for a rehearsal if they are to be in the procession.

First communion candidates

In addition to rehearsing the procession, the candidates will want to have some understanding of the important purpose of the procession. Catechists and families can help the candidates un-

■ To Memorize

GREETING

Presider: In the name of the Father, and of the Son, and of the Holy Spirit.

Candidate (*makes the sign of the cross and answers*): Amen.

Presider: The Lord be with you.

Candidate: And also with you.

Greetings
(from the sacramentary)

The grace of our Lord Jesus Christ and the love of God and the fellowship of the Holy Spirit be with you all.

The grace and peace of God our Father and the Lord Jesus Christ be with you.

The Lord be with you.

After the entrance song, the priest and the whole assembly make the sign of the cross. Then through his greeting the priest declares to the assembled community that the Lord is present. This greeting and the congregation's response express the mystery of the gathered Church (GIRM 28).

derstand this by drawing on their experience of parades. Younger candidates have a sense that parades are important. Ask them to think about how the opening procession is like a parade.

Sign of the Cross, Greeting, Introduction

Purpose

The purpose of this part of the liturgy is to say who we are. We are a people marked by the cross of Christ. We are a people filled with the Spirit of the Lord, who is always with us.

Planning Comments

 There are three choices for the greeting. The choice is not as important as the tone and feeling with which the greeting is offered.

The introduction is optional and is perhaps best omitted at the first communion liturgy. Everyone *knows* we are gathered to celebrate this important day for the first communion candidates. If an introduction is given, it should be concise and brief. The chances of the introduction being done well improve dramatically if it is written out beforehand.

Some presiders add an informal greeting at this point. There is a difference between an *introduction* and a *greeting*. The liturgy provides a formal greeting and allows for an introduction. There is no provision in the liturgy for an informal greeting such as "Good morning." Adding an informal greeting only further burdens an already wordy section of the liturgy without adding anything of significance.

 Be careful of adding more words.

Role of the Assembly

The role of the assembly is to make the sign of the cross and to respond to the greeting in a sincere, heartfelt manner.

Role of the First Communion Candidates

It is important that the candidates also respond fully to signify their readiness to participate in this liturgy.

Preparation

Pastoral planning team

The catechist can help prepare for this moment by always beginning the preparation session with the sign of the cross. The catechist will also want to help the candidates reflect on the central meaning of the cross for our faith. It can be difficult for younger candidates to fully grasp the theology of the cross, but it is the cross they are accepting when they accept communion. It is essential for the catechist to help the candidates understand what this means for them.

If the catechist also uses the greetings from the sacramentary during the catechetical sessions, the candidates will become familiar with the ritual dialogue.

The pastoral planning team can help prepare for this moment by writing, critiquing, and revising the introduction. They can help the presider decide if an introduction is even necessary. If there is to be an introduction, the presider will want to rehearse it out loud a few times before the liturgy.

Parish

The parish can help prepare by modeling active participation in making the sign of the cross and responding enthusiastically to the greeting at the community liturgies.

First communion families

The first communion families can prepare by practicing the sign of the cross at the beginning of all home prayers. They can also practice the three different greetings from the sacramentary in their home prayers.

First communion candidates

It will help the candidates to prepare if they understand the meaning of the sign of the cross. It may also be helpful if they understand that the greetings we use at Mass come from Scripture. The first greeting is from 2 Corinthians 13:13; the second is from Galatians 1:3 and other Pauline letters; the third is from Ruth 2:4.

Penitential Rite and Sprinkling Rite

Purpose

The purpose of the penitential rite is often misunderstood. It is not about confessing our sins so that we may be "pure" before beginning the liturgy. The penitential rite is never to be an examination of conscience, as happens when presiders begin the litany with the phrase "For the times we have ..., Lord have

■ To Memorize

SPRINKLING RITE

The candidate makes the sign of the cross as he or she is sprinkled with holy water.

■ To Memorize

PENITENTIAL RITE

A. Confiteor

Candidate:
I confess to almighty God,
and to you, my brothers
  and sisters,
that I have sinned
  through my own fault
in my thoughts and
  in my words,
in what I have done,
and in what I have failed
  to do;
and I ask blessed Mary,
  ever virgin,
all the angels and saints,
and you, my brothers
  and sisters,
to pray for me to the Lord
  our God.

Presider:
May almighty God
  have mercy on us,
forgive us our sins,
and bring us
  to everlasting life.

Candidate: Amen.

B. Kyrie

Presider: Lord, have mercy.

Candidate: Lord,
have mercy.

Presider: Christ, have mercy.

Candidate: Christ,
have mercy.

Presider: Lord, have mercy.

Candidate: Lord,
have mercy.

SPRINKLING RITE

Option B

Dear friends,
this water will be used
to remind us of our baptism.
Let us ask God to bless it,
and to keep us faithful
to the Spirit he has given us.

Lord God almighty,
creator of all life,
of body and soul,
we ask you to bless +
  this water:
as we use it in faith
forgive our sins
and save us from all illness
and the power of evil.

Lord,
in your mercy
give us living water,
always springing up
  as a fountain of salvation:
free us, body and soul,
  from every danger,
and admit us to your
  presence
in purity of heart.

Grant this through Christ
  our Lord.

(Amen.)

(After the sprinkling:)

May almighty God cleanse
  us of our sins,
and through the eucharist
  we celebrate
make us worthy to sit
  at his table
in his heavenly kingdom.

(Amen.)

mercy." The penitential rite in general and the Kyrie in particular are moments of joy in which we recognize that we are consumed by the overwhelming mercy of God. (See Daniel P. Grigassy, OFM, "Penitential Rite at Mass," *Dictionary of Sacramental Worship*.)

Planning Comments

There are three major options for the penitential rite. The team may also choose to do the sprinkling rite instead of the penitential rite.

 The sprinkling rite is the most obvious choice for the first communion liturgy since it most clearly recalls our baptism.

Baptism is a sacrament of initiation and Eucharist is the culmination of our initiation. Since the first communion candidates will be fully participating in the eucharistic banquet for the first time at this liturgy, it is important to recall their celebration of baptism.

Role of the Assembly

The role of the assembly is to participate fully in the responses to the invocations and to sing robustly the song that accompanies the sprinkling.

 Some members of the assembly might also participate by doing the sprinkling. Nothing in the sacramentary indicates that the presider is the only one who may sprinkle the assembly.

Role of the First Communion Candidates

The role of the candidates is to imitate the members of the assembly in their active participation in this rite. It would not be appropriate for the first communion candidates to actually do the sprinkling.

Preparation

Pastoral planning team

The catechist can help prepare for the sprinkling rite by helping the candidates understand the link between this part of the liturgy and their baptism. Part of the preparation process might include bringing the candidates to one of the regular parish baptism liturgies.

The pastoral planning team can prepare by helping to select from among the three prayer options for the sprinkling rite.

 Option B in the sacramentary may be the most appropriate choice for first communion. Option C may be appropriate if first communion is celebrated in the Easter season.

The pastoral planning team will also want to help by being sure the sprinkling ritual is well rehearsed. This is even more important if members of the assembly will be helping with the sprinkling. If the ritual will be done differently than at an ordinary liturgy, the presider will also want to be at the rehearsal.

Parish

The parish can help prepare for this ritual by celebrating a sprinkling rite at all liturgies that have some initiatory character to them. This would especially be the case during the Easter season.

First communion families

First communion families can practice using water blessings in their home prayer and by using occasional family meals as times to reflect on the initiatory aspects of baptism and meal sharing.

First communion candidates

Candidates can prepare for this moment by participating in parish baptisms—either as relatives or simply as members of the assembly. Some of the candidates might also help assemble the materials for the sprinkling such as evergreen branches and bowls.

Gloria

Purpose

The Gloria was originally intended to lend solemnity to the Christmas liturgy, and then only one at which a bishop presided. Over time, the use of the Gloria was gradually extended so that since the twelfth century it has been used at all Sunday and feastday liturgies.

The restricted use of the *Gloria*, i.e., only on Sundays outside Advent and Lent and on solemnities and feasts (GI, no. 31), emphasizes its special and solemn character (MCW 66).

■ To Memorize

GLORIA

Glory to God in the
   highest,
and peace to his people
   on earth.

Lord God, heavenly King,
almighty God and Father,
we worship you, we give you
   thanks,
we praise you for your glory.

Lord Jesus Christ, only Son
   of the Father,
Lord God, Lamb of God,
you take away the sin
   of the world:
have mercy on us;
you are seated at the right
   hand of the Father:
receive our prayer.

For you alone are the
   Holy One,
you alone are the Lord,
you alone are the Most High,
   Jesus Christ,
   with the Holy Spirit,
   in the glory of God
      the Father. Amen.

Planning Comments

 The Gloria must be sung because it is a hymn. To merely recite it is almost worse than not doing it at all.

However, to sing an opening hymn, a song during the sprinkling, and then a Gloria is a pastoral and liturgical difficulty. The U.S. bishops have approved a revision to the sacramentary that would make the use of the Gloria (and the penitential rite) optional. That revision is still awaiting approval by Rome at the time of this writing. A pastoral solution in the meantime might be to either sing the Gloria as the opening hymn or to sing it during the sprinkling rite.

Here are some suggested settings for the Gloria:

◆ "Gloria" from *Mass of Creation*, Marty Haugen

◆ "Gloria," Judy Hylton

◆ "Gloria" from *Mass of the Bells*, Alexander Peloquin

◆ "Gloria," John Foley, SJ

Role of the Assembly

The role of the assembly is to fully participate in the singing of the Gloria. This should not be a "choir piece."

Role of the First Communion Candidates

Likewise the candidates are to participate fully in the singing.

Preparation

Pastoral planning team

The catechist can help prepare for this part of the liturgy by encouraging the candidates to memorize the Gloria. A sung Gloria could also be used as part of the prayer during some of the catechetical sessions.

The pastoral planning team can help prepare by scheduling a Gloria in the music selections that the candidates can learn and enjoy singing throughout the preparation time.

Parish

The parish can help by participating in the Gloria when it is sung at Sunday Masses in order to help the candidates learn the song.

Next the priest invites the people to pray and together with him they observe a brief silence so that they may realize they are in God's presence and may call their petitions to mind. The priest then says the opening prayer, which custom has named the "collect." This expresses the theme of the celebration and the priest's words address a petition to God the Father through Christ in the Holy Spirit.

The people make the prayer their own and give their assent by the acclamation, **Amen** (GIRM 32).

First communion families

First communion families can get a copy of the Gloria text and use it as a family prayer and as a basis for faith-sharing.

First communion candidates

Candidates can prepare by learning the Gloria that will be sung at the first communion liturgy and by reflecting on the meaning of the text.

Opening Prayer

Purpose

The opening prayer is, along with the opening song, the most important part of the opening rites. It is the moment when we turn to God, finally gathered as a community, and ask God to prepare our hearts for hearing the word and celebrating the Eucharist.

Planning Comments

Two opening prayers are available for any Sunday liturgy. The first is a translation from the original Latin sacramentary. The second is an original composition in English. The choice of the prayer should be made by keeping in mind the best option for the formation of the candidates.

The opening prayer is the climax of the opening rites. However, it is often lost in the complexity of all the elements of this part of the Mass. Make the prayer more prominent by allowing for a good period of silent prayer right after, "Let us pray." The prayer can also be enhanced by good and careful proclamation by the presider.

Also note that the opening prayer may be sung or chanted. This was much more common before the Second Vatican Council. Chanting the opening prayer lends a sense of solemnity and festivity to the liturgy. The celebration of first communion might be an appropriate time for the presider to chant the opening prayer.

Role of the Assembly

The role of the assembly is to pray intently as the presider speaks the prayer and to answer with a faith-filled "Amen."

Role of the First Communion Candidates

The role of the candidates is to concentrate on the words of the prayer and to do their best to offer the prayer sincerely along with the presider and the other members of the assembly.

Preparation

Pastoral planning team

The catechist can help prepare for this moment in the liturgy by helping the pastoral team decide well ahead of time what opening prayer will be used. This prayer can then be made part of the prayer during catechetical sessions.

The pastoral planning team can help prepare by giving input into the choice of the prayer. The presider can prepare by reading or chanting the prayer out loud several times before the liturgy. A well-rehearsed, sincerely prayed oration can be a powerful moment of formation in any liturgy. This is even more true in the first communion liturgy.

 It would be a grave disservice to the candidates to simply pick an opening prayer on the spot and read it unrehearsed.

Parish

No particular preparation is required of the parish. However, the parish could, as part of its regular adult catechesis, spend some set of weeks during the year learning about the history of the opening prayer and sharing faith over a prayerful reading of some of the prayers in small group sessions.

First communion families

First communion families can prepare by getting a copy of the opening prayer that will be used at the first communion liturgy and reflecting on its meaning.

First communion candidates

Candidates can prepare for this moment by participating in the family faith-sharing over the prayer previous to the first communion liturgy. They can also practice concentrating on the opening prayers at Sunday Masses during their preparation period.

Opening Song

St. Augustine said to sing is to pray twice. That may be why the first action of the liturgy is a song. You may have heard people say that first impressions are very important. That is certainly true in the liturgy. Many times you can judge how well the liturgy will go by how well the opening song goes.

As a catechist, you may sometimes have some say in what the opening song will be for special children's liturgies and perhaps for the first communion liturgy. Usually, however, the parish musicians choose the opening song. Your primary job is to catechize the first communion candidates about the importance and purpose of the opening song.

Young candidates do not need to know the entire liturgical purpose and theological explanation of the opening song. They do need to know, however, that it is very important that they participate in the singing of it. The reason it is so important is because it is the very first act we do together as a worshiping community. It is our way of saying, "Okay, God, we're all together and all of us are ready to pray now."

The opening song also has an evangelistic quality to it. On almost any occasion, there is a stranger or a newcomer in our midst as we gather to worship. That newcomer is checking us out. We may not always know that somebody new is there, so we have to discipline ourselves to be conscious of the possibility. Whenever we have a guest present, we want to show ourselves at our best. So every time we gather to worship, we will want to sing our best, right from the start.

As a catechist, you can help the first communion candidates enter more deeply into the opening song by singing some of the opening songs during your sessions. If you don't feel confident in your singing ability, ask one of the parish musicians to make a tape of some of the opening songs for the coming weeks. Then have everyone sing along to the tape.

You can also catechize the candidates by reflecting on the song. Ask the candidates to read the text out loud without the music. Ask them to point out the most interesting or the most confusing phrases. Ask them why they think the parish would be singing that particular song to start the liturgy. Sometimes the words may be too complicated for younger candidates to understand. If that is the case, ask them to share how the song makes them feel when they sing it.

Penitential Rite and Sprinkling Rite

The penitential rite in the Mass, one of the newest additions to the liturgy, is often misunderstood. The penitential rite was added to the Mass after the reform of the Second Vatican Council. It blends the penitential prayers at the foot of the altar that the priest used to say in the pre-Vatican II liturgy and the Kyrie eleison.

"Kyrie eleison," which translates into "Lord, have mercy," is not of itself a penitential statement. It can mean "Lord forgive us," but it can also mean "Praise God, because God is compassionate." The latter better captures the sense of the way the original Kyrie eleison was used in the liturgy. It was an acclamation of praise that accompanied a procession.

What makes the penitential rite seem more like penance than praise are three things: the title of the rite, the (often spontaneous) introduction to the rite by the presider, and the choice of invocations that accompany the Kyrie.

The sacramentary gives three options for the introduction, and permission is given for adapting the text using "similar words." The third option, concluding with "let us call to mind our sins," is the least appropriate but perhaps most often chosen option. The purpose of the introductory rites is "to make the assembled people a unified community and to prepare them properly to listen to God's word and celebrate the eucharist" (GIRM 24). Stopping in the middle of that process to call to mind our individual sins seems to work at cross purposes with the goal of this part of the liturgy.

Similarly, invocations that begin with the phrase, "For the times that ..., Lord, have mercy," turn us inward and inhibit the action of joining with one another in communal worship.

The catechist and the liturgy planning team need to always ask themselves, "Do we want to begin the Mass with a penitential rite?" On some occasions, particularly in Lent, the answer may be yes. But this part of the liturgy does not have to be penitential if the focus of the celebration is not penitential.

Particularly in the case of the first communion liturgy, which is not celebrated in a penitential season, it makes more sense to choose to do the sprinkling rite—which replaces the penitential rite—because of its echoing of the candidates' initiation. First communion is the culmination of the initiation process they began in baptism.

If you choose not to do a sprinkling rite, you can still do the Kyrie and focus more on the praise aspect of the rite. Use Option A as a model for the introduction, adapting it to focus more clearly on God's compassion. Choose invocations from the sacramentary that clearly reflect the mood of the day. There are nine options in all. You also have the option of writing your own, using those in the sacramentary as a model.

Opening Prayer

The opening prayer is the most important part of the opening rites and is also the oldest. St. Justin mentions it in a second-century account of the liturgy.

This prayer is important because it is our first prayer addressed to God. It is our way of asking God to be with us as we worship and to prepare us to hear God's word. Part of your task as a catechist will be to impress upon the first communion candidates how important this prayer is. It can sometimes be difficult for young candidates to pay attention, but this is a prayer that they will want to try their hardest to focus on.

One thing that can help is to ask the presider to chant the prayer. Chanting the opening prayer was much more common before the Second Vatican Council, but now it has almost died out. The musical sound of the words might help to enchant the younger candidates and keep their attention.

On any Sunday, there are two opening prayers to choose from. The first is a translation from the original Latin. The second is a new English composition that was written after the Second Vatican Council. When the new sacramentary is approved in a few years, there will be four choices for each Sunday. The first will be the translation from the Latin. The next three will be new compositions which reflect the readings for each cycle of the liturgical year.

As the catechist, you can have some input into which prayer is chosen. Have your pastor or liturgy director give you a copy of the prayer choices for the Sunday that first communion will be celebrated. Have the first communion candidates read the prayers out loud. Ask them to talk about phrases that are interesting or difficult to understand. Ask them how each of the prayers makes them feel. Based on their responses, you and the candidates can recommend to the liturgy planning team which prayer you would like to use for the first communion liturgy.

You can also send copies of the prayer you choose home with the candidates so they can share the prayer with their families. Be sure to get copyright permission before doing this. The rights to all the prayers in the sacramentary are held by the International Commission on English in the Liturgy (1522 K St., NW, Suite 1000, Washington, DC 2005; 202-347-0800).

PART TWO

Liturgy of the Word

Liturgy of the Word

Overview

The Liturgy of the Word is the point in the liturgy when God calls us to faith. We believe God's word is a living word and not a history lesson or only a story about events that happened long ago. Through the proclamation of the Scriptures and the homily, God speaks to us as a community, asking us to follow the cross.

Outline of the Rites

- First Reading
- Responsorial Psalm
- Second Reading
- Alleluia or Gospel Acclamation
- Gospel
- Homily
- Profession of Faith
- Prayer of the Faithful

Catechist Background Sheets

- The Readings
- The Homily
- The Intercessions
- Adapting Liturgy of the Hours for Home Prayer and Preparation Sessions
- Sample Outline for Evening Prayer
- Sample Outline for Morning Prayer

Recommended Reading

Johnson, Lawrence J. "Liturgy of the Word." *The Word and Eucharist Handbook*. Rev. ed. (San Jose: Resource Publications, Inc., 1993). 28 ff.

Jungmann, Josef A. "The Service of Readings." *The Mass of the Roman Rite: Its Origins and Development*. 2 vols. Translated by Francis A. Brunner. New York: Benziger Brothers, Inc., 1951. Reprint (2 vols. in 1), revised and abridged by Charles K. Riepe, *The Mass of the Roman Rite*, Westminster, Md.: Christian Classics, Inc., 1978. Restored to 2 vols., 1986. 391-494.

Readings from scripture are the heart of the liturgy of the word. The homily, responsorial psalms, profession of faith, and general intercessions develop and complete it. In the readings, God speaks to his people and nourishes their spirit; Christ is present through his word. The homily explains the readings. The chants and the profession of faith comprise the people's acceptance of God's Word. It is of primary importance that the people hear God's message of love, digest it with the aid of psalms, silence, and the homily, and respond, involving themselves in the great covenant of love and redemption. All else is secondary (MCW 45).

"Liturgy of the Word." *The Mystery of Faith* (Washington, DC: Federation of Diocesan Liturgical Commissions, 1981). 27-49.

Wagner, Nick. "What are some ways to make our lectors better proclaimers?" and "What is the connection between the Liturgy of the Word and the Liturgy of the Eucharist?" *Modern Liturgy Answers the 101 Most-Asked Questions about Liturgy*. San Jose: Resource Publications, Inc., 1996. 32, 38.

First and Second Readings

Purpose

The purpose of the first and second readings is two-fold. First, they speak to us in their own right, telling us what God has in mind for us. Second, they give context to and highlight the Gospel. The first two readings must always be understood in light of the Gospel.

Planning Comments

If first communion takes place at a Sunday liturgy, the readings of that Sunday must be used. If a votive Mass is chosen, more options are available.

The lectors for first communion are ordinarily the regular parish lectors, even at a votive Mass. For a liturgy this important, the parish wants the best trained, most skilled lectors in the community. If one of the family members is a trained lector, he or she might be asked to proclaim the readings.

Sometimes an untrained parent or even one of the candidates is asked to proclaim the readings. This is usually done with the goal of making the candidates or the families feel more involved. It often has just the opposite effect, though. An untrained lector or someone who is too young to effectively proclaim the readings cannot proclaim the word in such a way that the assembly can hear the reading clearly, nor can he or she proclaim the reading in a way that moves the assembly to faith. Proclamation is a community-oriented skill that takes much work to master. At a liturgy as important as first communion, the assembly needs the best the community has to offer.

The many riches contained in the one word of God are admirably brought out in the different kinds of liturgical celebrations and liturgical assemblies. This takes place as the unfolding mystery of Christ is recalled during the course of the liturgical year, as the Church's sacraments and sacramentals are celebrated, or as the faithful respond individually to the Holy Spirit working within them. For then the liturgical celebration, based primarily on the word of God and sustained by it, becomes a new event and enriches the word itself with new meaning and power. Thus in the liturgy the Church faithfully adheres to the way Christ himself read and explained the Scriptures, beginning with the "today" of his coming forward in the synagogue and urging all to search the Scriptures (LMIn 3).

The Liturgy of the Word also requires some silence to allow the word to echo in our hearts. Plan for a good period of silence after each reading.

If the first communion liturgy is not being celebrated on a Sunday or major feastday, you may choose the readings for the liturgy. Here are some suggested Scriptures for the first and second readings.

Old Testament

- Genesis 14:18–20
- Genesis 15:1–6,18
- Genesis 17:1–8
- Genesis 35:1–4,6–7
- Exodus 16:2–4,12–15
- Exodus 24:3–8
- Deuteronomy 8:2–3;14–16
- Deuteronomy 30:15–20
- Joshua 24:1–2,15–25
- 1 Kings 19:4–8
- 2 Kings 5:9–15
- Proverbs 9:1–6
- Isaiah 44:1–3
- Jeremiah 31:31–34

New Testament

- Acts 2:42–47
- Acts 2:14,36–40,41–42
- Acts 8:26–38
- Acts 10:34–43
- Romans 6:3–11
- Romans 8:28–39
- 1 Corinthians 10:16–17
- 1 Corinthians 11:23–26
- 1 Corinthians 12:12–13
- Galatians 3:26–28
- Ephesians 1:3–14
- Ephesians 4:1–6
- Colossians 3:9–17
- Titus 3:4–7
- Hebrews 9:11–15
- Hebrews 10:22–25
- 1 Peter 2:4–10
- Revelation 19:1,5–9

Role of the Assembly

The role of the assembly in this part of the liturgy is to actively listen to God's word as it is proclaimed through the readings. This is a difficult task that is mastered only with practice. It is different than listening to the television or the radio. It is more like listening as the pilot of an airliner listens to the control tower when there is some difficulty with landing the plane. Important things are at stake both on the airliner and in the liturgy.

Role of the First Communion Candidates

The candidates may not be as skilled at listening as are their elders in faith. Nevertheless, their role is to master the art of listening as best they can and take the word of God to heart.

■ To Memorize

RESPONSE TO READINGS

Lector (*at the conclusion of the reading*): The Word of the Lord.

Candidate: Thanks be to God.

This unique and very important song [the responsorial psalm] is the response to the first lesson. The new lectionary's determination to match the content of the psalms to the theme of reading is reflected in its listing of 900 refrains. The liturgy of the Word comes more fully to life if between the first two readings a cantor sings the psalm and all sing the response. Since most groups cannot learn a new response every week, seasonal refrains are offered in the lectionary itself and in the *Simple Gradual*. Other psalms and refrains may also be used, including psalms arranged in responsorial form and metrical and similar versions of psalms, provided they are used in accordance with the principles of the *Simple Gradual* and are selected in harmony with the liturgical season, feast or occasion. The choice of the texts which are not from the psalter is not extended to the chants between the readings (NCCB, Nov. 1968; cf. GI, No. 6). To facilitate reflection, there may be a brief period of silence between the first reading and the responsorial psalm (MCW 63).

Preparation

Pastoral planning team

The catechist will want to prepare for this part of the liturgy by making sure the candidates know the distinction between the Old Testament and the New Testament. They should also have some knowledge of who St. Paul is, since so many of the readings are taken from his letters. The catechist will also want to use liberal amounts of Scripture throughout the preparation process.

The role of the pastoral planning team is to make sure there is an adequate lector training program available so the first communion liturgy planners will have competent ministers to assist with this part of the liturgy.

If the pastoral planning team has chosen regular parish lectors for the first communion liturgy, it will probably not be necessary to remind them to rehearse their readings several times, out loud, well before the liturgy. However, if the team is unsure of the lectors' commitment, it is up to the team to meet with the lectors and help them with their rehearsal. Always keep in mind that the presider is also a lector in the liturgy and no less preparation is required of him.

Parish

The parish prepares for this part of the liturgy by demonstrating over the course of the preparation time for the first communion candidates (and indeed, over the whole life of the parish) that they take the readings to heart every Sunday. By the time of the first communion liturgy they will have shown by their example how the first communion candidates are to understand and put into action the readings they will hear at this liturgy.

This does not need to seem like some idealistic, far-off goal that we hope our parishes will one day realize. Most Catholics are faithful, good-hearted people who put their belief into action every day. What is often missing is some explicit connection between that action and what is proclaimed on Sunday. It is not too difficult to imagine a simple faith-sharing process—perhaps paralleling the first communion preparation—in which small groups of parishioners gather to tell one another how they go about living out God's call.

First communion families

If gathering the parish as a whole to share faith over the Sunday Scriptures is too difficult, at least the first communion families should gather. Every week, in some form or another, they will benefit from sharing faith with one another. The sessions do not need to be long and complicated. Each session should, in some form or another, deal with the question, "How do we go about living out God's call as heard in the readings this week?"

First communion candidates

The candidates prepare for this part of the liturgy by sharing faith weekly over the Sunday readings. This may be the most essential element of their preparation. Many well-intentioned parish leaders and families want to ensure the candidates "know enough" about the faith without first ensuring that the candidates *have* faith. While the facts of the faith are important and ought not be neglected, faith itself is primary and is all that is required for celebrating first communion.

Psalm and Alleluia

Purpose

The purpose of the psalm between the readings is to give a sense of the emotion or spirit of the liturgy. The purpose of the alleluia is to lift our hearts in joy and praise as we get ready to hear the Gospel.

Planning Comments

Both the psalm and the alleluia should be sung. The rubrics do allow for the psalm to be recited on occasion, but it is difficult to imagine why this compromise would be allowed at a Sunday liturgy or at a first communion liturgy. There is no instance in which the alleluia may be recited. If it is not sung, it is to be omitted. In the season of Lent, the alleluia is replaced by another Gospel acclamation. Some psalms that may be appropriate for the liturgy include:

- Psalm 23 (The Lord is my shepherd)
- Psalm 34 (Taste and see the goodness of the Lord)
- Psalm 78 (The Lord gave them bread from heaven)
- Psalm 116 (The cup of salvation I will take up)
- Psalm 145 (The hand of the Lord feeds us)
- Psalm 147 (Glorify the Lord, O Jerusalem)

Some suggested alleluia settings include:

- "Celtic Alleluia," Christopher Walker
- "Joyful Alleluia," Howard Hughes
- "Alleluia" from *Mass of the Bells*, Alexander Peloquin
- "Alleluia" from *Mass of Creation*, Marty Haugen

[The alleluia, an] acclamation of paschal joy is both a reflection upon the Word of God proclaimed in the liturgy and a preparation for the gospel. All stand to sing it. After the cantor or choir sings the alleluia(s), the people customarily repeat it. Then a single proper verse is sung by the cantor or choir, and all repeat the alleluia(s). If not sung, the alleluia should be omitted (GI, No. 39). A moment of silent reflection may be observed in its place. During Lent a brief verse of acclamatory character replaces the alleluia and is sung in the same way (MCW 55).

Role of the Assembly

The role of the assembly is to participate in these parts of the proclamation of the word by giving their full voice and heart to the singing.

Role of the First Communion Candidates

The role of the candidates is to follow the example of the assembly, singing as fully as possible.

Preparation

Pastoral planning team

The catechist will want to prepare for these parts of the liturgy by making the psalms a regular part of his or her personal prayer. In addition, the catechist will want to know how the church has used the psalms in the daily morning and evening Liturgy of the Hours and how that prayer can be adapted for use in the preparation sessions.

The pastoral planning team prepares for these parts of the liturgy by ensuring that the parish has an adequate repertoire of psalmody and Gospel acclamations that can be sung well, without rehearsal.

The pastoral planning team also provides for competent music ministers who can plan and lead these musical moments.

The team also determines if there will be a Gospel procession during the alleluia. If so, it will usually require rehearsal.

Parish

The parish prepares for these parts of the liturgy by growing in their understanding of the great liturgical and pastoral significance of the responsorial psalm. With the help of the parish leadership, the parish can come to understand the psalms as the prayer of the church, and they will be able to pass on that understanding to the first communion candidates. Creative parish leaders will be able to think of a number of ways to make the significance of the psalms apparent to the parish. The easiest and most obvious is to do the psalm well every Sunday. Another is to make broader use of the Liturgy of the Hours. Another is to use a schedule of seasonal responsorial psalms in the Mass, accompanied by a short paragraph in the Sunday bulletin about the particular psalm in use. A short brainstorming session with the pastoral team will yield more ideas.

First communion families

First communion families can prepare for these moments in the liturgy by learning the role of psalms and acclamations in the liturgy. They can also spend time praying the psalms at home.

■ To Memorize

RESPONSE TO THE GOSPEL

Presider or deacon (*at the beginning of the Gospel*): The Lord be with you.

Candidate: And also with you.

Presider or deacon: A reading from the holy gospel according to ____.

Candidate: Glory to you, Lord.

The candidate, using the right hand, then makes the sign of the cross on his or her forehead, lips, and heart.

Presider or deacon: (At the conclusion of the Gospel) The gospel of the Lord.

Candidate: Praise to you, Lord Jesus Christ.

In addition, the first communion families prepare by actively participating in the singing of the psalm and the Gospel acclamation at every liturgy in order to provide an example for the candidates.

First communion candidates

Candidates prepare for these moments by memorizing some of the more important psalms chosen by the catechetical team. They can be encouraged to pray these and other psalms as a regular part of their spiritual discipline. One of the psalms memorized should be the one that will be sung at the first communion liturgy.

In addition, the candidates should know a few of the parish Gospel acclamations by heart, especially the one that will be sung at the first communion liturgy.

Gospel and Homily

Purpose

The reading of the Gospel is the high point of the Liturgy of the Word. Everything in the liturgy so far—particularly the proclamation of the previous readings—is supposed to prepare the assembly for this moment.

The Gospel, along with the other biblical readings, is the living word of God. We know that it is actually God speaking when the Scriptures are proclaimed. And we know that every time God speaks, something happens. God's word is creative. What happens in the Sunday assembly when God speaks—when the readings are proclaimed—is that people come to deeper faith.

The proclamation of the Gospel is the moment *par excellence* when God speaks most clearly to us.

The purpose of the homily is to help us better understand how our faith shapes the way we see the world and the way we act in the world. For this reason, the homily is not a talk given *during* the liturgy. The homily is part of liturgy itself. The homily serves as a bridge between the Liturgy of the Word and the Liturgy of the Eucharist, showing us how we put the faith we have received into action.

Planning Comments

The Gospel is always proclaimed in such a way as to make clear its climactic nature in the Liturgy of the Word. At the very least,

Contemporary ecclesiology provides a second and even more fundamental reason for beginning with the assembly rather than with the preacher or the homily. *The Dogmatic Constitution on the Church* describes the church as the mystery of God's saving will, given concrete historical expression in the people with whom he has entered into a covenant. This church is the visible sacrament of the saving unity to which God calls all people. "Established by Christ as fellowship of life, charity, and truth, the church is also used by Him as an instrument for the redemption of all, and is sent forth into the whole world as the light of the world and the salt of the earth" (#9). The church, therefore, is first and foremost a gathering of those whom the Lord has called into a covenant of peace with himself. In this gathering, as in every other, offices and ministries are necessary, but secondary. The primary reality is Christ in the assembly, the People of God (FIYH 5).

A homily preparation group can also be formed by gathering the priests in the rectory, the parish staff, priests from the area, priest and ministers, or a priests' support group. The presence of members of the congregation in a group is especially helpful in raising issues that are of concern to them and which the homily may be able to address. Groups that involve only clergy or parish staff members can also be a rich source of insight into the ways in which the Scriptures point to the continuing presence of God in human history (FIYH 107).

this means preceding the proclamation with an acclamation and standing for the reading. However, on solemn occasions there might also be a separate Gospel procession complete with candles and incense. Also, the Gospel might be sung. If the entire Gospel is not sung, the introductory material ("The Lord be with you" and "A reading from the holy Gospel...") and the concluding material ("The Gospel of the Lord") could be sung.

The homily is to flow from the readings or from one of the elements or prayers of the liturgy. The challenge of the homilist for the first communion liturgy is to not let the homily become a "talk" to first communicants. They homilist will want to make clear that the Eucharist is a Gospel event. Also plan for a good deal of silence after the homily.

If the first communion liturgy is not celebrated on a Sunday or major feast, you can choose from among these Scriptures for the Gospel:

- Mark 14:12–16,22–26
- Luke 24:13–35
- John 6:24–35
- John 6:51–58
- Luke 9:11–17
- John 5:1–15
- John 6:41–51
- John 21:1–14

Role of the Assembly

 The starting place of the homily is with the assembly.

The gathered assembly *is* the Body of Christ. The first role of the assembly is to live up to this responsibility, becoming as fully as possible the reality of Christ to each other and to the world. As the assembly attempts to meet this challenge, frustrations will surface, faith will lag, and difficulties will arise. Likewise, victories will be won, joy will increase, and courage will be gained. It is, then, also the role of the assembly to make known to the homilist these struggles and successes, so when the liturgy is celebrated the homilist can communicate effectively to the assembly about faith in Christ.

Role of the First Communion Candidates

The role of the candidates is to follow the example of the assembly, living out the faith of Christ and making known to the homilist the challenges and joys of that faith.

Preparation

Pastoral planning team

The catechist can prepare for this part of the liturgy by helping the candidates understand the significance of the Gospel in the life of faith. The catechist will want to make sure the candidates have a sense of the four different Gospel writers. The catechist can also prepare the candidates to understand the role of the Gospel in the liturgy and the ritual actions that surround its proclamation.

The pastoral planning team as a whole prepares by being good listeners, growing in their understanding of the faith lives and needs of the community. The team, and particularly the presider, will also want to spend a good deal of preparation time with the homily. The homilist will want to spend a significant amount of time and energy preparing for this moment. In the frenzied world of modern parish life, it is very difficult to find time to allow for adequate homily preparation. However, it is the Sunday homily that has the greatest impact on the greatest number of people in the pastoral ministry of the homilist. The U.S. bishops' document *Fulfilled in Your Hearing* outlines an excellent process for involving members of the parish in the homily preparation. The process outlined there might be adapted to involve the first communion families in the homily preparation.

In addition, the person who will proclaim the Gospel (usually the same person as the homilist) will want to practice the reading out loud several times.

Parish

The parish prepares for this moment in the first communion liturgy by reading and praying over the Sunday readings—especially the Gospel—ahead of time. The homily has a greater impact when the parish understands the readings and some of the faith questions they raise.

First communion families

We have already spoken of the need for first communion families to gather in weekly faith-sharing groups to pray over the Sunday readings. If time is limited, the faith-sharing groups will want to focus their energies on the Gospel reading.

These faith-sharing groups might also serve, with the help of the parish pastoral planning team, as homily preparation groups as discussed in *Fulfilled in Your Hearing*. If this is not possible throughout the entire preparation process, it could at least be facilitated for the first communion liturgy.

First communion candidates

The candidates prepare for this part of the liturgy by following the example of their elders to the best of their ability. This would

The ... profession of faith in the celebration of Mass serves as a way for the people to respond and to give their assent to the word of God heard in the readings and through the homily and for them to call to mind the truths of faith before they begin to celebrate the eucharist (GIRM 43).

■ To Memorize

NICENE CREED

We believe in one God,
the Father,
the Almighty,
maker of heaven and earth,
of all that is seen
and unseen.

We believe in one Lord,
Jesus Christ,
the only Son of God,
eternally begotten of
the Father,
God from God,
Light from Light,
true God from true God,
begotten, not made,
one in Being
with the Father.
Through him all things
were made.
For us men and for our
salvation
he came down from heaven:

(All bow during these two
lines:)

by the power of the
Holy Spirit
he was born of the
Virgin Mary,
and became man.

For our sake he
was crucified
under Pontius Pilate;
he suffered, died,
and was buried.
On the third day he
rose again in fulfillment
of the Scriptures;
he ascended into heaven
and is seated at the right
hand of the Father.
He will come again in glory
to judge the living and
the dead,
and his kingdom will have
no end.

We believe in the
Holy Spirit, the Lord,

mean at the very least reading the Gospel before Mass every week (or having it read to them) and finding one idea in the Gospel to focus on during the week and during the liturgy.

We cannot expect younger candidates to be able to comprehend the entire Gospel and homily each week. But, with practice, they ought to be able to learn how to take away one idea from the homily that seems important to them. This information should be communicated back to the homilist either formally through a homily preparation group process or informally as first communion families encounter the homilist at parish events.

Profession of Faith and Prayer of the Faithful

Purpose

The purpose of the profession of faith (also called the creed) is to reaffirm our baptismal commitment which has been recalled more deeply in the Liturgy of the Word and which we are about to celebrate in the Liturgy of the Eucharist.

The purpose of the prayer of the faithful (also called the general intercessions) is for the assembly to exercise its priestly function of praying for the needs of the world. It is the first action of the assembly flowing directly from the Liturgy of the Word.

Planning Comments

When large numbers of candidates are present at a liturgy, the Apostles' Creed may be used instead of the Nicene Creed. However, if the candidates do not know the Apostles' Creed by heart, it may be better to use the more familiar Nicene Creed.

The general intercessions are to be prayers for the church, the world, the oppressed, and the local community. They are not to be prayers of thanksgiving or prayers for the specific needs of individuals.

The intercessions can be sung by the cantor or deacon instead of being recited to lend an air of festivity and solemnity to the liturgy.

It is important to remember that the prayer of the faithful is actually the prayer of the community, written by someone in the community, and not taken verbatim from a commercial publication.

Role of the Assembly

The prayer of the faithful is the only prayer of the liturgy in which the assembly actually offers the prayer themselves. It is very important, therefore, that they do so with their whole heart and their whole mind.

Role of the First Communion Candidates

It is generally *not* a good idea to have several of the first communion candidates read the intercessions. Younger candidates are usually not very good at speaking in public. In addition, they will be nervous on this important occasion. It is more pastorally sensitive to allow them to focus on participating as members of the assembly.

Preparation

Pastoral planning team

The catechist prepares for this part of the liturgy by making intercessory prayer a regular part of the preparation sessions and helping the candidates grow in their ability to pray.

The pastoral planning team prepares for this moment in the liturgy by discerning the needs of the church, the world, the oppressed, and the local community. The team then either prepares the intercessions or arranges for a competent member of the parish to do so.

Parish

The parish prepares by becoming involved in the concerns of the church, the world, the oppressed, and the local community so they know what needs to be prayed for. Then, the prayer of the faithful will have profound meaning in the liturgy.

First communion families

First communion families would be involved in the concerns of the groups prayed for along with the rest of the parish. However, during the preparation period they would want to be even more diligent in their involvement in order to make clear to the candidates the connection between prayer and action.

The families might also be involved in preparing the petitions. During the preparation sessions they might be divided into separate petition groups (church, civil world, oppressed, salvation of the world, sick, initiates, etc.), and each group would be responsible for a petition from their area.

the giver of life,
who proceeds from
the Father and the Son.
With the Father and the Son
he is worshiped
and glorified.
He has spoken through
the Prophets.
We believe in one holy
catholic and apostolic
Church.
We acknowledge one
baptism for the
forgiveness of sins.
We look of the resurrection
of the dead,
and the life of the world
to come. Amen.

In the general intercessions or prayer of the faithful, the people, exercising their priestly function, intercede for all humanity. It is appropriate that this prayer be included in all Masses celebrated with a congregation, so that petitions will be offered for the Church, for civil authorities, for those oppressed by various needs, for all people, and for the salvation of the world (GIRM 45).

■ To Memorize

PRAYER OF THE FAITHFUL

The response to the prayer of the faithful varies, but the most common one, which the candidate should learn, is, "Lord, hear our prayer."

First communion candidates

The first communion candidates can spend some of their preparation period memorizing the Nicene and Apostles' Creeds if they have not already learned them. They would further benefit from a faith-sharing session, along with their families, on the words and meaning of the creed. This does not need to be very complicated. They could, for example, be asked the baptismal questions ("Do you believe in God the Father," etc.). After each "I do," they could be asked why they believe that. Or, they could be asked to draw pictures about what they believe.

The candidates can also prepare by learning who we pray for in the prayer of the faithful and why we pray for these groups. They can pray for the same groups in their daily prayer during their preparation period. If they are involved in the concerns of these groups along with their families, their prayer will have profound meaning for the candidates.

The Readings

The readings proclaimed at Mass come from the lectionary. ("Lection" means "lesson" or "reading.") The lectionary was revised after the Second Vatican Council, which mandated that "the treasures of the Bible ... be opened up more lavishly, so that a richer share in God's word may be provided for the faithful" (CSL 51).

The Sunday readings are arranged on a three-year cycle. Each cycle is based on one of the first three Gospels—Matthew (Year A), Mark (Year B), and Luke (Year C). Because the Gospel of John is written in a very different style from the first three, it does not have its own cycle. Parts of John are read throughout the other cycles, especially in Year B.

The Old Testament readings in each cycle were chosen because they somehow harmonize with the message of the Gospel. The New Testament readings, in ordinary time, are not purposefully harmonious with the Gospel reading. The New Testament readings are chosen in a "semi-continuous" fashion, meaning passages are read straight through over the course of the Sundays.

In most cases, the focus of the liturgy and of the homily is derived from the Gospel. When preparing the candidates for first communion, it is important to keep the Gospel message in mind. The more that you are able to help the candidates grasp the message of the Gospel, the more meaningful the first communion celebration will be for them.

The preparation of the candidates begins with your own preparation. Well before your preparation sessions with the candidates, you may want to spend some time praying over the readings that will be used for the first communion celebration—especially the Gospel. It will help you understand the Gospel more deeply if you look up the passage in a Bible. Read the passage in the context of the larger story. What is happening before and after the passage? Why do you think the Gospel writer wrote what he did? Why do you think the church will be proclaiming the passage on the particular liturgical day for which it is scheduled?

Most Bibles have good footnotes and introductory comments to the Gospels. Reading these can help you understand the passage more deeply. If you have access to a good biblical commentary, that can also be helpful but is not absolutely necessary.

You will no doubt learn a great deal more than you can possibly communicate to the first communion candidates. But the more prepared you are, the more sure you will be in your preparation with the candidates.

The Homily

Catechists and other liturgical planners tend to think of the homily as "Father's job." This is a mistake. The U.S. bishops wrote a document about homilies in which they said, "We believe that it is appropriate, indeed essential, to begin this treatment of the Sunday homily with the assembly rather than with the preacher" (FIYH 4). The fundamental reason for beginning with the assembly is that "the primary reality is Christ in the assembly, the People of God" (5). All the ministries of the assembly, including that of the homilist, are important, but secondary.

Simply stated, a homily that comes solely "from" Father and is delivered "to" the assembly will fail. The homily must begin in and come from Christ, who is in the assembly.

During the homily of the first communion liturgy, there may be a temptation to "instruct" the candidates in the assembly. This is the way many adults are used to dealing with children. While younger candidates no doubt need instruction, and while a homily can certainly be instructive, instruction is not the primary purpose.

"Rather the homily is preached in order that a community of believers who have gathered to celebrate the liturgy may do so more deeply and more fully—more faithfully—and thus be formed for Christian witness in the world" (FIYH 43).

Your challenge as a catechist is to first of all ask yourself if you know how to do this. Do you know how to call the first communion candidates to celebrate the liturgy more deeply, fully, and faithfully?

Of course you do. It is no secret and there is no trick to it. Think first of all of your own experience of liturgy. What kinds of liturgy move you the most deeply? When have you felt the most involved? When have you felt as though you were getting a foretaste of the heavenly banquet?

These have likely been times when the symbols were clear, the music was familiar and powerful, the ritual action was smooth, and the preaching was "right."

To understand right preaching, keep in mind that the homily is not a talk given on the occasion of a liturgical service. It is not a speech nor a lesson. It is a part of the liturgy itself—flowing from the word, leading to the Eucharist. The homily is to both remind us of our faith and call us to deeper faith in the word just proclaimed. The homily calls us to profound thanksgiving—*eucharistia*—for God's saving, faithful word.

Your challenge as a catechist is to know what right preaching is so you can avoid asking the homilist to "speak to the children." Instead, your goal is to challenge the homilist to call the candidates and the entire assembly to celebrate the liturgy more deeply, fully, and faithfully.

The Intercessions

The prayer of the faithful (or general intercessions) is prayed directly to God by the members of the assembly. Therefore, the full, conscious, and active participation of the assembly is very important at this point in the liturgy.

Children can be good prayer writers. The images they use are direct and concrete. As their catechist, you can help them draw images from the readings and from the liturgy itself as they compose prayers of intercession. These prayers can be used in their preparation sessions, in their home prayer, and, with enough planning, even in the first communion liturgy. Having the candidates help write the prayers is a better way to involve them in this part of the liturgy than having several of them line up at the microphone during the liturgy, each one nervously speaking a different prayer.

Here are some specific guidelines:

1. The presider introduces the prayer of the faithful with a *short* introduction. For example: "Let us now offer our prayer to the Lord." The presider concludes the prayer of the faithful with a collect addressed to God. The collect is ideally sung.

2. The intercessions themselves are addressed to the assembly in one of three forms:

a. "For _____."
b. "That _____."
c. "For _____, that _____."

The form should remain consistent throughout the prayer. Of the three, the first is preferable because it tends to be shorter, less preachy, and less wordy. The least preferable is the "For _____, that _____" form because it is usually longer, preachier, and wordier. Always avoid the use of the word "especially" when writing intercessions.

3. The sequence of the intercessions follows the order listed in the *General Instruction of the Roman Missal* (46), which is "a. for the needs of the church; b. for public authorities and the salvation of the world; c. for those oppressed by any need; [and] d. for the local community." In addition, it is customary to pray for the dead as the final intercession.

4. The prayer of the faithful is always petitionary. This is not the place for prayers of thanksgiving.

5. The prayer of the faithful is always public; therefore it is not appropriate to conclude the petitions with something like, "For your individual prayers, which we now offer silently." Nor is it appropriate to pray for "special intentions."

6. It is the role of the deacon to proclaim the intercessions. In the absence of a deacon, another member of the assembly can proclaim them. It is not ideal to have one member of the assembly perform the role of two different ministers. Therefore, it is not ideal to have the presider proclaim the intercessions. His job is to preside. Likewise, it is not ideal to have the lector proclaim the intercessions. It is his or her job to proclaim the readings. Nor is it ideal to have some of the first communion candidates proclaim the prayer. Their job is to be first communicants.

7. As a general rule, the intercessions are sung, but they may be spoken.

8. Keep it short. Keep sentences short, and keep the number of intercessions short.

Please remember, these guidelines will carry you only so far. Don't get so caught up in the rules that you lose sight of the goal. That is, the prayer of the faithful is intended to be a passionate prayer that touches everyone at the deepest level possible. If you can do that, everything else will fall into place.

Adapting Liturgy of the Hours For Home Prayer and Preparation Sessions

Praying the psalms is an excellent way to prepare the candidates for their first communion. The *General Instruction on the Liturgy of the Hours* says the Liturgy of the Hours is in itself the best preparation for the celebration of the Eucharist (12).

Individual members of the faithful have, from the very early days of the church, set aside time for prayer. The most common times were at the end of the day (dusk), the beginning of the day, and the middle of the day (noon). The prayer they prayed at each of these times was probably the Lord's Prayer. Soon, these individuals began to come together for common prayer at set hours of the day, most commonly evening and morning. These are still the primary hours of prayer for Christians. Over time, more hours of prayer became common, and a schedule of psalms was assigned to the hours of prayer.

In our history, there are two traditions of the Liturgy of the Hours, which is also called the Divine Office. One tradition is the people's prayer or "cathedral" tradition. In this tradition, there was more of a focus on evening and morning as the central hours of prayer. The cathedral tradition was simple to celebrate and emphasized the ritual. Every evening the people would pray Psalm 141 (My prayers rise like incense, my hands like an evening offering). Every morning they would pray Psalm 63 (You are my God, whom I seek). The people would pray other psalms and canticles and make other prayers, but these two psalms were and are the core of the cathedral tradition.

The other form of the Liturgy of the Hours is the "monastic" tradition. The focus in the monasteries was to pray at several set times during the day (dawn, morning, midday, noon, mid-afternoon, evening, night) and, over the course of a month, to pray all 150 psalms. There was not as much focus on ritual; there was more of an effort to interiorize the message of the psalms. When priests and religious speak today of "praying the office," this is the tradition they are speaking of.

The cathedral tradition is more appropriate and more accessible for most Catholics today. When developing a cathedral-style Liturgy of the Hours, keep the following in mind:

◆ Christ is truly present when we celebrate the Liturgy of the Hours and he accomplishes his priestly work of redeeming humankind, just as he does in the Eucharist (GILH 13).
◆ The Liturgy of the Hours is a foretaste of the praise that resounds in heaven (GILH 16).
◆ This celebration is *liturgy* and is therefore subject to all the requirements of good liturgy, especially the full, conscious, and active participation of the faithful.
◆ The celebration of the hours of evening and morning are symbolic of Christ's descent into the tomb at sunset and his resurrection at sunrise.
◆ The Liturgy of the Hours also celebrates and sanctifies chronological time. It is in balance with the Sunday Eucharist, which celebrates *kairos* time or time beyond time.

◆ The Liturgy of the Hours has a two-part structure: praise and petition. The praise portion is made up of psalms and canticles. The petition portion is made up of intercessions and the Lord's Prayer.

◆ The Liturgy of the Hours, like the Eucharist, is meant to be a sung prayer.

Sample Outline for Evening Prayer

Invitation to Prayer
[The leader lights a candle and says or sings]

Leader: Light and peace in Jesus Christ our Lord.

All: Thanks be to God.

Hymn
[The *Phos Hilaron*—an ancient evening hymn found in most hymnals—is traditionally sung. However, any evening song will do. Two common ones are "All Creatures of Our God and King" and "Day Is Done."]

Psalmody
Psalm 141 [It is customary to incense the candle, the Word, and the assembly while this psalm is sung.]

[Second Psalm]
[A second psalm may be sung. Other evening psalms include 19, 23, 27, 84, 91, 104, 117, 118, 121, 122, 130, and 145.]

Reading

Gospel Canticle
[At Evening Prayer, the *Magnificat* (Lk 1:46–55) is sung.]

Intercessions

Lord's Prayer

Dismissal
Leader: May the Lord bless us, + protect us from all evil, and bring us to everlasting life.

All: Amen.

Sample Outline for Morning Prayer

Invitation to Prayer

Leader: O God, + come to my assistance.

All: Lord, make haste to help me.

Leader: Glory to the Father, and to the Son, and to the Holy Spirit.

All: As it was in the beginning, is now, and will be forever. Amen. (Alleluia.)

Hymn

[Sing any morning hymn. Some of the more common ones are "Morning Has Broken," "All Creatures of Our God and King," "All People That on Earth Do Dwell," and "Joyful, Joyful, We Adore You."]

Psalmody

Psalm 63

[Second Psalm]

[A second psalm may be sung. Other morning psalms include 5, 8, 33, 42, 66, 72, 80, 85, 93, 95, 98, 100, 118, 148, 149, and 150.]

Reading

Gospel Canticle

[At Morning Prayer, the *Benedictus* (Lk 1:68–79) is sung.]

Intercessions

Lord's Prayer

Dismissal

Leader: May the Lord bless us, + protect us from all evil, and bring us to everlasting life.

All: Amen.

PART THREE

Liturgy of the Eucharist

Communion Rite

Liturgy of the Eucharist

Overview

The Liturgy of the Eucharist is our response to God's word. No matter what the readings are, every Liturgy of the Word calls us to follow Christ more fully and completely. The ultimate expression of our faithful "yes" to God's call is to become one with Christ in the sharing of his body and blood.

Outline of the Rites

- Preparation of the Altar and Gifts
- Prayer over the Gifts
- Eucharistic Prayer
    - Opening Dialogue
    - Preface
    - Acclamation (Holy, Holy, Holy)
    - Epiclesis (Invocation of the Holy Spirit)
    - Institution Narrative (Consecration)
    - Memorial Acclamation
    - Anamnesis (Remembrance)
    - Offering
    - Intercessions
    - Final Doxology
    - Great Amen
- Communion Rite

Catechist Background Sheets

- Understanding the Preparation of Gifts
- Faith-Sharing Questions for Eucharistic Prayer III

Recommended Reading

Johnson, Lawrence J. "Liturgy of the Eucharist." *The Word and Eucharist Handbook*. Rev. ed. San Jose: Resource Publications, Inc., 1993. 64 ff.

Jungmann, Josef A. "The Sacrifice." *The Mass of the Roman Rite: Its Origins and Development*. 2 vols. Translated by Francis A. Brunner. New York: Benziger Brothers, Inc., 1951. Reprint (2 vols. in 1), revised and abridged by Charles K. Riepe, *The Mass of the Roman Rite*, Westminster, Md.: Christian Classics, Inc., 1978. Restored to 2 vols., 1986. Vol. 2, 1–274.

LaVerdier, Eugene. *Dining in the Kingdom of God: The Origins of the Eucharist According to Luke*. Chicago: Liturgy Training Publications, 1994.

"Liturgy of the Eucharist." *The Mystery of Faith*. Washington, DC: Federation of Diocesan Liturgical Commissions, 1981. 53 ff.

Wagner, Nick. "What is the connection between the Liturgy of the Word and the Liturgy of the Eucharist?"; "How should we handle second collections?"; "When are we supposed to kneel during Mass?"; "Why does the priest mix water with the wine before the eucharistic prayer?"; "Why does the priest wash his hands before the eucharistic prayer?" *Modern Liturgy Answers the 101 Most-Asked Questions about Liturgy*. San Jose: Resource Publications, Inc., 1996. 38–42.

Preparation of Altar and Gifts

Purpose

The purpose of the preparation of gifts is to present the fruits *of* the community *to* the community for offering in the eucharistic prayer.

Planning Comments

While the preparation of gifts is an important part of the liturgy, it is not a primary part and ought not be overdone.

There is a liturgical principle which says that the weaker parts of the liturgy tend to acquire more elaboration as time goes on. This makes some sense if you think about it. It is difficult to "add" something to the eucharistic prayer because that prayer is so central and so sacred to the liturgy. So, if a liturgy planning team wants to add something creative to the liturgy, they might be tempted to turn to a "less sacred" moment such as the preparation of gifts. (The time after communion is another such moment.) Resist this temptation.

The preparation of gifts must be kept simple and direct so as not to distract from the more important action of the eucharistic prayer. The only gifts to be brought to the altar are the bread and wine and the monetary collection.

It is fitting for the faithful's participation to be expressed by their presenting both the bread and wine for the celebration of the eucharist and other gifts to meet the needs of the Church and of the poor.

The faithful's offerings are received by the priest, assisted by the ministers, and put in a suitable place; the bread and wine for the eucharist are taken to the altar (GIRM 101).

The eucharistic prayer is preceded by the preparation of the gifts. The purpose of the rite is to prepare bread and wine for the sacrifice. The secondary character of the rite determines the manner of the celebration. It consists very simply of bringing the gifts to the altar, possibly accompanied by song, prayers to be said by the celebrant as he prepares the gifts, and the prayer over the gifts. Of these elements the bringing of the gifts, the placing of the gifts on the altar, and the prayer over the gifts are primary. All else is secondary (MCW 46).

When the bread and wine are brought forward, they are brought directly to the altar by the members of the community. The presider stands at the altar and does not come down to meet them at the sanctuary step.

This action may take place in silence or may be accompanied by instrumental music or a song. The song may be sung by the entire assembly or it may be a solo piece performed by the choir or the cantor. If music of any kind accompanies the ritual, however, it *must* end when the ritual ends. If the presider is waiting at the altar for the song to finish, we have changed the function of music as serving the liturgy into music being served by the liturgy.

At solemn liturgies, it is appropriate to incense the gifts and the assembly during the preparation rites. If you decide to do this, be sure the music is planned accordingly to cover the extra time.

This is also the point in the liturgy when the collection takes place. If the liturgy is on a Sunday, be sure to check that a second collection is not scheduled. Taking up a second collection for various needs is an over-used device that is usually harmful to the liturgy and to the total dollar amount collected.

Role of the Assembly

The role of the assembly in this part of the liturgy is to provide for the bread and wine—either through their monetary contributions or by making these gifts themselves—and to present the gifts at the altar. The assembly also contributes to *itself* by providing for the funding of parish activities and staffing through the collection. In addition, some provision should be made for a contribution to the needy. In many communities, this is done by a parish-wide agreement that some portion of the collection will be donated to those in need. If the first communion liturgy is not one of the regular Sunday liturgies, the total collection would ordinarily be given to the needy.

Role of the First Communion Candidates

The role of the candidates is to make some contribution as well. They might prepare the bread for this liturgy. They would certainly contribute to the collection basket. If the candidates are children, they may have allowances. Those who don't have an allowance do have access to many resources by relying on their parents. It should be clear to the first communion candidates that part of their role in the eucharistic assembly will be to deny themselves some small portion of their material goods so that the money saved can be contributed to the parish. Even in communities where the families are truly poor, the first communicants can contribute some of their time to helping the parish or the other needy people in their community.

■ To Memorize

PREPARATION OF GIFTS

Priest:
Blessed are you, Lord,
  God of all creation.
Through your goodness
  we have this bread
  to offer,
which earth has given
  and human hands
  have made.
It will become for us
  the bread of life.

Candidate: Blessed be God forever.

Priest:
Blessed are you, Lord,
  God of all creation.
Through your goodness
  we have this wine to offer,
fruit of the vine and work
  of human hands.
It will become our
  spiritual drink.

Candidate: Blessed be God forever.

Priest:
Pray, my brothers
  and sisters,
  that our sacrifice
may be acceptable to God,
  the almighty Father.

Candidate:
May the Lord accept
  the sacrifice at your hands
for the praise and glory
  of his name,
for our good, and the good
  of all his church.

It is often better *not* to have the candidates present the gifts at this liturgy. They already have a primary role—that of first communion candidates. It would be appropriate, however, to have the candidates, along with their families, present the gifts throughout the Sundays of their preparation period.

Preparation

Pastoral planning team

The catechist prepares for this part of the liturgy by understanding exactly what is going on during the preparation of gifts. The preparation of gifts is what some might call a "weak" moment in the liturgy. Because of that, the focus of this moment can be easily lost. By understanding the purpose of the preparation of gifts, the catechist will be better able to prepare the candidates and better able to help prepare the liturgy. (See the catechist handout on page 75 for more information.)

The liturgy planning team prepares for this part of the liturgy by ensuring that enough bread and wine is available for the liturgy. In addition, the team assures that some members of the community are willing take up the collection and to present the gifts. If those bringing up the gifts have not performed this role before, the team will need to arrange for a rehearsal.

If music is to accompany this part of the ritual, the liturgy planning team should see to it that the musicians know this and that they plan appropriate music.

Parish

The parish prepares for this moment in the liturgy by determining ahead of time how the needs of the less fortunate will be met through the collection.

First communion families

The first communion families prepare for this moment by making a commitment to the financial support of the parish and by contributing to the needs of the poor. This commitment ought to be made through prayer and consultation with the candidates. In families whose resources are scarce, the candidates would ideally have some say in what family "fringes" are sacrificed for the sake of the larger community.

If the first communion celebration does not take place during one of the regular Sunday liturgies, families might be involved in determining which charity the collection would be donated to. They could also spend time during the preparation process becoming involved in the work of that charity.

First communion candidates

Candidates prepare for this part of the liturgy by also making a commitment to the support of the parish in addition to the family contribution. If a candidate is unable to make a monetary commitment, he or she can be encouraged to make a time commitment.

In addition, the first communion candidates might prepare the bread for the liturgy. This can be done in the context of their families or—with some adult supervision—in their peer groups.

Eucharistic Prayer

Purpose

The purpose of the eucharistic prayer is to give praise and thanksgiving to God for all the works of creation and most especially for sending Jesus to save us from death. "Eucharist" comes from a Greek word that means "thanksgiving."

By praying the eucharistic prayer, we memorialize or remember Jesus' sacrifice for us. We do this throughout the entire prayer, but it is most evident when we sing the "memorial" acclamation.

By memorializing or remembering Jesus' sacrifice, the sacrifice becomes present and real for us. By our remembering, we become one with Jesus and with Jesus' sacrifice.

The bread and wine that we have offered to the Father also become for us that Jesus-sacrifice. They become the Body and Blood of Jesus, sacrificed for us, and will be broken, poured out, and shared for our sakes.

Planning Comments

There are nine different eucharistic prayers to choose from for Sunday liturgies, plus another Eucharistic Prayer for Masses for Various Needs and Occasions which can be used on other days.

1. Eucharistic Prayer I is the English translation of the Roman Canon. The Roman Canon was the only eucharistic prayer used in the Roman Catholic liturgy during the middle ages and up until the Second Vatican Council.

2. Eucharistic Prayer II is the English translation and adaptation of an ancient prayer from the early third century. It is said to have been written by Hippolytus, who was the pope at that time.

3. Eucharistic Prayer III is an original prayer composed in English after the Second Vatican Council.

The meaning of the [eucharistic] prayer is that the entire congregation joins itself to Christ in acknowledging the great things God has done and in offering the sacrifice (GIRM 54).

■ To Memorize

OPENING DIALOGUE

Priest: The Lord be with you.

Candidate: And also with you.

Priest: Lift up your hearts.

Candidate: We lift them up to the Lord.

Priest: Let us give thanks to the Lord our God.

Candidate: It is right to give him thanks and praise.

The eucharistic prayer, a prayer of thanksgiving and sanctification, is the center of the entire celebration. By an introductory dialogue the priest invites the people to lift their hearts to God in praise and thanks; he unites them with himself in the prayer he addresses in their name to the Father through Jesus Christ. The meaning of the prayer is that the whole congregation joins itself to Christ in acknowledging the works of God and in offering the sacrifice (GI, No. 54). As a statement of the faith of the local assembly it is affirmed and ratified by all those present through acclamations of faith: the first acclamation or Sanctus, the memorial acclamation, and the Great Amen (MCW 47).

■ To Memorize

HOLY

Holy, holy, holy Lord,
God of power and might,
heaven and earth are full
of your glory.
Hosanna in the highest.

Blessed is he who comes
in the name of the Lord.

Hosanna in the highest.

4. Eucharistic Prayer IV is based on ancient eucharistic prayers from the eastern rite.

5. In 1974, three eucharistic prayers for children were approved.

6. In 1975, two eucharistic prayers for reconciliation were approved.

7. In 1995, the Eucharistic Prayer for Masses for Various Needs and Occasions was issued.

It is important to remember that the eucharistic prayer begins with the preface. The preface is the part that begins with the dialogue: "The Lord be with you." "And also with you." It immediately precedes the Holy.

There are eighty different prefaces. Depending on the day you choose to celebrate first communion, you may have a choice among prefaces to use. Some eucharistic prayers have a fixed preface that must always be used with that prayer.

Since the eucharistic prayer is a single element in the liturgy, the acclamations (Holy, Memorial, Amen) are most appropriately all of one musical composition.

On solemn occasions, the eucharistic prayer may be sung or chanted from start to finish. On less solemn occasions, the opening dialogue and perhaps the preface might be sung.

Some acclamation settings for the eucharistic prayer include:

◆ *Mass of Creation*, Marty Haugen

◆ "Land of Rest," adapted by Marcia Pruner

◆ *St. Louis Jesuits Mass*, Bob Dufford, SJ, and Dan Shutte

◆ *Mass of Thanksgiving* (based on "Simple Gifts"), Richard Jeffrey

Role of the Assembly

This can be the most difficult part of the liturgy for the assembly to feel engaged in. The eucharistic prayer is by its nature a prayer proclaimed by a single presider.

Nevertheless, this prayer belongs to the entire assembly as the presider not only speaks in our name, but from within the midst of the assembly and as one with the assembly.

The importance of this prayer requires that the presider proclaim it in a strong, clear voice. The prayer also requires the concentrated attention of the assembly, focusing intently on the prayer.

Role of the First Communion Candidates

 If there are large numbers of children at the first communion liturgy, it may be appropriate to use one of the eucharistic prayers for children. These prayers are written in a language that can be more engaging to children. Also, there are more options within these prayers for sung acclamations from the children and the assembly, which will help the children participate more fully in the prayer.

Preparation

Pastoral planning team

The catechist prepares for this part of the liturgy by understanding the structure of the eucharistic prayer and its role in the liturgy. This can be something of a struggle. However, in order effectively prepare the candidates, it is important to be a familiar and comfortable as possible with this important part of the liturgy.

The liturgy planning team can prepare for this part of the liturgy by carefully selecting which eucharistic prayer will be prayed at this liturgy. They will want to consider the images within each prayer that most clearly reflect the faith-journey of the candidates and their families.

The presider will want to prepare for this part of the liturgy by rehearsing the prayer out loud, even if it is very familiar. The challenge will be to find a way of proclaiming the prayer in a new way that particularly emphasizes the images and phrases that might be important to the candidates and their families.

The musicians will want to choose acclamations for the prayer that unify the prayer and that will be sung well by the assembly.

 The first communion liturgy is not a good time to try a new Holy, Memorial Acclamation, and Amen.

Parish

The parish can best prepare for this moment by finding ways to explore the history, meaning, and purpose of the eucharistic prayer. The eucharistic prayer is much more than a lengthy prelude to the "consecration." It is when we pray this prayer under the leadership of an ordained presider that we most clearly identify ourselves as Catholics. An active parish will want to

[The Holy] is the people's acclamation of praise concluding the preface of the eucharistic prayer. We join the whole communion of saints in acclaiming the Lord. Settings which add harmony or descants on solemn feasts and occasions are appropriate, but since this chant belongs to priest and people, the choir parts must facilitate and make effective the people's parts.

We support one another's faith in the paschal mystery, the central mystery of our belief. [The memorial] acclamation is properly a memorial of the Lord's suffering and glorification, with an expression of faith in his coming. Variety in text and music is desirable.

The worshipers assent to the eucharistic prayer and make it their own in the Great Amen. To be most effective, the Amen may be repeated or augmented. Choirs may harmonize and expand upon the people's acclamation (MCW 56–58).

If possible, the acclamations should be sung by the children rather than recited, especially the acclamations that form part of the eucharistic prayer.

The eucharistic prayer is of the greatest importance in the eucharist celebrated with children because it is the high point of the entire celebration. Much depends on the manner in which the priest proclaims this prayer and on the way the children take part by listening and making their acclamations. The disposition of mind required for this central part of the celebration and the calm and reverence with which everything is done must make the children as attentive as possible. Their attention should be on the real presence of Christ on the altar under the elements of bread and wine, on his offering, on the thanksgiving through him and with him and in him, and on the Church's offering, which is made during the prayer and by which the faithful offer themselves and their lives with Christ to the eternal Father in the Holy Spirit (DMC 30, 52).

explore what it is about this prayer that makes us Catholic and what it is about this prayer that prevents us from celebrating Eucharist when we cannot pray it.

First communion families

First communion families can prepare for this part of the liturgy by reading and praying over the eucharistic prayer that will be used during the first communion liturgy. The families can be encouraged to locate words and phrases that indicate thanksgiving, sacrifice, banqueting, remembering (memorial), and praise. Families can discuss what they believe to be the meaning and purpose of the eucharistic prayer.

First communion candidates

Beyond the faith-sharing the candidates will do with their families, they can make the preface that will be used in the first communion liturgy part of their daily prayer the week before first communion.

Communion Rite

Overview

The communion rite begins the climax of everything the first communion candidates have prepared for since baptism. Joining the community at the paschal banquet is the fulfillment of their baptism. The *Rite of Christian Initiation of Adults* says of the newly baptized: "Finally the eucharist is celebrated and for the first time the neophytes have the full right to take part. This is the culminating point of their initiation" (217).

Originally, the communion rite was very simple. It included only the breaking of the bread (without the singing of the Lamb of God) and the sharing of the bread and cup. These remain the two most important elements of the communion rite. Other ritual elements were added over time.

Outline of the Communion Rite

◆ Lord's Prayer

◆ Sign of Peace

◆ Fraction Rite (Breaking of Bread)

◆ Communion and Communion Song

◆ Song after Communion

◆ Prayer after Communion

Catechist Background Sheet

◆ Wheat-and-Water Only Bread Recipe

Recommended Reading

"Communion Rite." *The Mystery of Faith*. Washington, DC: Federation of Diocesan Liturgical Commissions, 1981. 92 ff.

Huck, Gabe. *The Communion Rite at Sunday Mass*. Chicago: Liturgy Training Publications, Inc., 1989.

Johnson, Lawrence J. "Communion Rite." *The Word and Eucharist Handbook*. Rev. ed. San Jose: Resource Publications, Inc., 1993. 102 ff.

Jungmann, Josef A. "The Communion Cycle." *The Mass of the Roman Rite: Its Origins and Development*. 2 vols. Translated by Francis A. Brunner. New York: Benziger Brothers, Inc., 1951. Reprint (2 vols. in 1), revised and abridged by Charles K. Riepe, *The Mass of the Roman Rite*, Westminster, Md.: Christian Classics, Inc., 1978. Restored to 2 vols., 1986. Vol. 2, 275–426.

The eating and drinking of the Body and Blood of the Lord in a paschal meal is the climax of our eucharistic celebration. It is prepared for by several rites: the Lord's Prayer with embolism and doxology, the rite of peace, breaking of bread (and commingling) during the "Lamb of God," private preparation of the priest, and showing of the eucharistic bread. The eating and drinking are accompanied by a song expressing the unity of communicants and followed by a time of prayer after communion (GI, No. 56). Those elements are primary which show forth signs that the first fruit of the Eucharist is the unity of the Body of Christ, Christians being loved by Christ and loving him through their love of one another. The principal texts to accompany or express the sacred action are the Lord's Prayer, the song during the communion procession, and the prayer after communion (MCW 48).

■ To Memorize

LORD'S PRAYER

Our Father,
who art in heaven,
hallowed be thy name;
thy kingdom come,
thy will be done on earth
as it is in heaven.
Give us this day
our daily bread;
and forgive us our
trespasses
as we forgive those
who trespass against us;
and lead us not
into temptation,
but deliver us from evil.

For the kingdom, the power,
and the glory are yours,
now and forever.

Lord's Prayer: this is a petition both for daily food, which for Christians means also the eucharistic bread, and for the forgiveness of sin, so that what is holy may be given to those who are holy. The priest offers the invitation to pray, but all the faithful say the prayer with him; he alone adds the embolism, *Deliver us*, which the people conclude with a doxology. The embolism, developing the last petition of the Lord's Prayer, begs on behalf of the entire community of the faithful deliverance from the power of evil. The invitation, the prayer itself, the embolism, and the people's doxology are sung or are recited aloud (GIRM 56a).

This Holy and Living Sacrifice: Directory for the Celebration and Reception of Communion under Both Kinds. Washington, DC: United States Catholic Conference, 1985.

Wagner, Nick. "Why do some parishes hold hands during the Our Father?"; What is the fraction rite?"; "What is meant by 'real bread' for Eucharist?"; "Why are churches taking out the tabernacle?"; "Why is it that some parishes do not give communion from the tabernacle?"; "Why should we receive communion from the cup?" *Modern Liturgy Answers the 101 Most-Asked Questions about Liturgy.* San Jose: Resource Publications, Inc., 1996. 43-50.

Lord's Prayer and Sign of Peace

Purpose

The purpose of the Lord's Prayer is preparation for communion. This is particularly due to the petition for our "daily bread" and the petition to "forgive us our trespasses."

St. Augustine spoke of the Lord's Prayer as being like washing the face before going to the altar (Jungmann 284).

The purpose of the sign of peace is to serve as an outward indication of unity and reconciliation with one another.

Planning Comments

The Lord's Prayer is also a prayer of unity. As such, it should be able to be prayed by everyone present. The Lord's Prayer ought to be known and prayed by heart. Memorizing the prayer is an important element of the communicants' preparation process.

The Lord's Prayer should not be sung unless the melody it is sung to is as familiar as "Happy Birthday" is to most people. If the tune in unfamiliar, some members of the assembly will be excluded from joining in the prayer.

The sign of peace is, within the structure of the communion rite, a relatively minor liturgical moment. However, it is sometimes over-emphasized to the detriment of the other elements of the rite. Remember that originally the communion rite consisted of only the fraction and the sharing. Conscientious liturgy planners will make these original elements the most significant.

That is not to say the sign of peace is unimportant or given less than its proper role. It helps to think of the sign of peace as a ritual dance. The sign of peace is not meant to *cause* reconciliation and unity so much as it is meant to give witness to it. In order to give proper witness, the sign of peace must be carried out with dignity and reverence.

If the participants in the liturgy are bilingual, they may be invited to pray in their native language.

It is generally not appropriate to hold hands during the Lord's Prayer. Holding hands is a duplication of both the sign of peace and communion itself. As such, it diminishes the power of both actions. However, if it is already the usual practice in your parish to hold hands during this prayer, it may be best not to confuse the candidates by trying to restrict them from doing so.

There is no song during the sign of peace, or even musical accompaniment. The action is brief, but solemn. The solemnity of the moment is lost if the assembly is spending time waiting for the presider or the musicians or other ministers to "complete their rounds."

Role of the Assembly

The assembly is a model for the first communion candidates. As such, they will want to pray the Lord's Prayer in a strong, clear voice. This is especially true of family members, guardians, and sponsors.

In a like manner, the assembly will share the peace with each other warmly and sincerely.

Role of the First Communion Candidates

The candidates may be nervous at this point. Praying the Lord's Prayer in a concentrated, intentional way can help calm them and reassure them of God's love.

To the extent they are able, the first communion candidates may want to focus on the connection of this prayer to their sharing in the Lord's heavenly banquet. After this day, they will never again be "hungry."

First communion candidates, like the rest of the assembly, will usually share the sign of peace with the two to four people nearest them in a prayerful fashion. It is not appropriate for the candidates to circuit the church as a way for everyone to get a look at them or greet them.

Preparation

Pastoral planning team

Catechists will want to be aware of the history of the Lord's Prayer. It was prayed three times a day by the early Christians as domestic or home-church prayer. It started being prayed in the eucharistic liturgy is some areas around the fourth century. It has not always been in the same place in the liturgy in every part of the world.

 The present placement of the Lord's Prayer in the Roman Rite was established in the sixth century by Pope Gregory the Great.

Catechists will also want to be aware of the connection of the Lord's Prayer to the initiation process. The Lord's Prayer was prayed at the baptism of the first communion candidates as a kind of foreshadowing and remote preparation for their communion at the Lord's table (RBC 181).

The *Rite of Christian Initiation of Adults* includes a special rite for "presenting" the Lord's Prayer to the catechumens. While this type of formal presentation might not be appropriate for baptized, catechized candidates preparing for first communion, becoming familiar with the rite can help the catechist better understand the initiatory significance of the prayer.

The planning team may want to be aware that the current sacramentary is being revised, and the sign of peace may eventually be permitted at another place in the liturgy. Most likely it will be an option to either leave it where it is or to move it to the conclusion of the Liturgy of the Word. The placement after the Liturgy of the Word is found in some ancient liturgies.

The team will also want to keep clear the distinction between the informal greeting that takes place in some parishes before Mass begins and the sign of peace. Some parishes have asked the assembly to shake hands and greet one another on a regular basis before Mass begins. This can be a helpful way of building community. However, it is important not to confuse it with the sign of peace.

 A before-Mass greeting is not a liturgical gesture and does not carry the ancient symbolism of unity and reconciliation that the sign of peace does.

Rite of peace: before they share in the same bread, the faithful implore peace and unity for the Church and for the whole human family and offer some sign of their love for one another.
The form the sign of peace should take is left to the conference of bishops to determine, in accord with the culture and customs of the people (GIRM 56b).

Parish

There are many ways the parish can prepare for the upcoming first communion by focusing on the Lord's Prayer. The simplest might be to ask parishioners at the beginning of Lent to pray the Lord's Prayer three times a day (morning, noon, and night) as the early Christians did. Their morning prayer might focus on the catechumens and infants who will be baptized in the current paschal season. Their noon prayer might focus on those being confirmed and those receiving first communion. And their evening prayer might focus on those returning to the church after being away for a time. Be sure to ask that the parish continue the practice throughout the Easter season as well.

Another, more direct preparation, is to ask the parish—on the Sunday before the first communion liturgy—to pray the Lord's Prayer often during the coming week as a support to the communicants. They might, for example, make the Lord's Prayer a part of their meal prayer or bedtime prayer. They might also pray it silently while waiting in lines or at stop lights.

First communion families

 Beyond what the parish as a whole is asked to do, first communion families might be asked to pray the Lord's Prayer three times daily from the moment their candidates begin their catechesis for first communion.

 Several times during the preparation period— or at least once during the paschal season— the families might meet together for an evening reflection on the Lord's Prayer.

 Families might also create a peace ritual to be celebrated at home on a regular basis or in times of conflict.

First communion candidates

The candidates will, of course, spend a significant amount of time memorizing the Lord's Prayer if they have not done so already.

Part of the catechesis for the first communion candidates would also include an extended reflection on the Lord's Prayer. This might be best done over several sessions by breaking the prayer into segments and asking the candidates to first recite the segment and then to draw pictures based on what they heard and saw in the prayer.

■ To Memorize

LAMB OF GOD

Lamb of God,
you take away the sins
of the world:
   have mercy on us.

Lamb of God,
you take away the sins
of the world:
   have mercy on us.

Lamb of God,
you take away the sins
of the world:
   grant us peace.

Holy communion has a more complete form as a sign when it is received under both kinds. For in this manner of reception a fuller light shines on the sign of the eucharistic banquet. Moreover there is a clearer expression of that will by which the new and everlasting covenant is ratified in the blood of the Lord and of the relationship of the eucharistic banquet to the eschatological banquet in the Father's kingdom (GIRM 240).

The nature of the sign demands that the material for the eucharistic celebration truly have the appearance of food. Accordingly, even though unleavened and baked in the traditional shape, the eucharistic bread should be made in such a way that in a Mass with a congregation the priest is able actually to break the host into parts and distribute them to at least some of the faithful. (When, however, the number of communicants is large or other pastoral needs require it, small hosts are in no way ruled out.) The action of the breaking of the bread, the simple term for the eucharist in apostolic times, will more clearly bring out the force and meaning of the sign of the unity of all in the one bread and of their charity, since the one bread is being distributed among the members of one family (GIRM 283).

First communion candidates might also be encouraged to practice the sign of peace. Some younger candidates may have little practice at shaking hands and looking directly at the person they are speaking to.

Fraction Rite

Purpose

The breaking of the bread and pouring out of the wine reminds us of Jesus' being "broken" on the cross and the shedding of his blood for our sakes. We see in the breaking of the bread our own brokenness.

Planning Comments

The breaking of the bread is one of the high points of the liturgy. It is important to create an atmosphere in which the assembly can focus on this action.

When the sign of peace is concluded and the communion ministers are in place, the presider takes one of the loaves and lifts it high over his head. He then tears the loaf in two.

 There should be no other movement or action happening in the church. When he tears the loaf, that is the signal for the musicians to begin the Lamb of God. It is also the signal for the communion ministers to step to the altar and assist the presider in breaking the rest of the loaves and in pouring out the wine.

 It is important to carefully follow the guidelines of *General Instruction of the Roman Missal* on the various aspects of the fraction rite. That means that the bread used for communion "must have been baked recently" (282) and "have the appearance of food"; it should be made in such a way that the priest can break it and distribute the parts (283).

The faithful share the body of the Lord in bread "consecrated at the same Mass" and not from the tabernacle. The assembly share the cup because in doing so communion "will stand out more clearly as sharing in the sacrifice actually being celebrated" (GIRM 56h).

If the community is not used to sharing bread consecrated at the same Mass and sharing from the cup, a good deal of preparation will be required of the liturgy team.

Communion ministers may also need to be rehearsed if the communion ritual will be different for the first communion candidates.

Role of the Assembly

The role of the assembly during the breaking of the bread and pouring out of the cup is to participate in the singing of the Lamb of God.

Role of the First Communion Candidates

The first communion candidates also sing the Lamb of God.

Preparation

Pastoral planning team

The catechist prepares for the fraction rite by growing in an understanding of the importance of the fraction rite. By understanding that it is in the breaking of the bread and the pouring out of the cup that the community comes to recognize Christ, the catechist will be better able to assist the candidates with their understanding of this climactic moment in the liturgy.

The pastoral planning team prepares for the fraction rite by ensuring that enough bread and wine are available for all in the assembly. If the communion ministers are not familiar with sharing communion from the cup, they will need some time to practice. If the communion ministers are not used to helping with the breaking of the several loaves of bread, they will need to practice that as well.

The musicians will want to choose an appropriate Lamb of God for the fraction rite. Since several loaves of bread are being broken, the Lamb of God will have to have a variable number of strophes. The musicians will also need to choose an appropriate song for the communion procession. Ideally, it will be one the assembly knows by heart so they will not need to have the words in front of them as the process to communion.

Parish

The parish has no particular preparation to make for this moment in the rite. However, their understanding of the fraction rite will deepen if the parish has some regular faith-sharing process in which the members of the community can reflect on their own "brokenness."

In a eucharistic celebration, the vessels for the bread and wine deserve attention and care (GI, Nos. 289–296). Just as in other types of celebration those objects which are central in the rite are a natural focus. When the eucharistic assembly is large, it is desirable not to have the additional plates and cups necessary for communion on the altar. A solution is to use one large breadplate and either one large chalice or a large flagon until the breaking of the bread. At the fraction, any other chalices or plates needed are brought to the altar. While the bread is broken on sufficient plates for sharing, the ministers of the cups pour from the flagon into the communion chalices. The number and design of such vessels will depend on the size of the community they serve. To eat and drink is of the essence of the symbolic fullness of this sacrament. Communion under one kind is an example of the minimizing of primary symbols (EACW 96).

After the prayer the priest genuflects, takes the eucharistic bread, and, holding it slightly above the paten while facing the people, says: *This is the Lamb of God.* With the people he adds, once only: *Lord, I am not worthy to receive you* (GIRM 115).

■ To Memorize

RESPONSE TO THE CALL TO COMMUNION

Lord, I am not worthy
   to receive you,
but only say the word
   and I shall be healed.

First communion families

Some of the first communion families can prepare for this part of the rite by baking the bread that is used in the ritual. [See catechist background sheet on page 79 for recipe].

All of the families can spend some time praying and sharing faith over the Lamb of God text. What does each family member see in that text? What does each one hear? What is the deep meaning of that text for each person?

First communion candidates

Candidates participate in the family preparation. In addition, they will want to memorize the Lamb of God so they can pray it with the rest of the assembly on the day of their first communion.

Call to Communion

Purpose

The purpose of the call to communion is to issue a formal invitation to the assembly share in the Lord's Supper. Some form of invitation exists in almost every liturgical tradition. In the Eastern Rite, the traditional call is "Holy things for the Holy."

Planning Comments

On this occasion, the call to communion might be adapted to incorporate the names of the first communion candidates (cf. RCIA 243).

After the bread has been broken and the wine has been poured, the communion ministers step back from the altar. The presider then asks the catechist to present those who will be coming to the table for the first time. As their names are called, each candidate steps into the center aisle and faces the altar. The presider holds out the bread and wine to the candidates and says: "This is the Lamb of God...."

The communion song begins *as soon as the people have responded:* "Lord, I am not worth to receive you, but only say the word, and I shall be healed." There should be no delay.

Role of the Assembly

The role of the assembly is to respond vocally and spiritually to the call to the table.

Role of the First Communion Candidates

If their names are called individually, the candidates step into the center aisle as they are called. In any case, their role is to respond vocally with the assembly and, for the first time, approach the table with joy and thanksgiving.

Preparation

Pastoral planning team

The catechist will want to prepare for this part of the rite by reflecting on the meaning of "call." It will be important for the catechist to assist the candidates in understanding what it means to accept the call to the table.

If the individual names are to be called, the catechist and the rest of the team will want to rehearse the ritual with the families and candidates.

The planning team will also want to rehearse the families and candidates in the ritual for sharing communion. A cup of water is usually used at the rehearsal in place of wine. However, it would be good to remind the families to have the candidates practice with a sip of wine at home, especially if the candidates are younger and have never tasted wine before. It is best to practice with a wine similar to that which will be used in the first communion liturgy. The taste of wines can vary a great deal.

The candidates will also need to practice holding their hands correctly to receive the consecrated bread.

 If there will be changes in the way first communion has been celebrated in the past, it will be important for the presider to be part of the rehearsal.

Parish

The parish has no particular preparation to make for this moment in the rite.

The children should not be allowed to forget that all the forms of participation reach their high point in eucharistic communion, when the body and blood of Christ are received as spiritual nourishment (DMC 22).

First communion families

 Families can prepare for the call to communion by asking friends and relatives to leave their cameras (both video and still) at home or in their cars. This is a ritual moment, not a Kodak moment. If we are going to be good models for the candidates, we must model for them that we believe communion to be one of the most important spiritual moments of our lives as Catholics. Distracting our prayer and the candidates' with flashing cameras does not give the proper message.

In addition, in preparation for communion, families will want to practice sharing bread and wine at home with the candidates several times before the liturgy.

First communion candidates

Candidates can prepare for this time by rehearsing the ritual with the catechist. Beyond this, the candidates will want to prepare by spending a good deal of time in prayer. This will be a time when they are likely to be nervous. Knowing that the Holy Spirit will be with them, giving them guidance and strength, can be a comfort to them.

Communion

Purpose

The purpose of communion is to make us one—one with Christ and one with each other. St. Augustine says, "That which you receive, that you yourselves are." The world is fractured by sin and death. Even we, the members of the faithful, separate ourselves from one another. Yet all that is overcome by Christ's death and resurrection. In sharing in his sacrifice, through the sharing of his body and blood, we are reconciled to him and to each other.

The purpose of communion is also to nourish is us. Our mandate is not only to overcome our own divisions and brokenness. We are commanded to go out into the world to heal the sin and brokenness that exists all around us. For this, communion gives us strength.

Planning Comments

The liturgical documents are clear that communion is a more complete sign when shared under both the forms of bread *and* wine (GIRM 240). It will be important to plan for this if it is not already regular parish practice.

 The liturgical documents also make clear that communion is not to be shared from the tabernacle. Some planning may need to take place if enough bread is not usually consecrated at each Mass for that assembly.

Many parishes celebrate the Mass of the Lord's Supper each Holy Thursday by using real bread for communion. It seems the celebration of first communion would be an even more appropriate occasion for this practice.

The *Rite of Christian Initiation of Adults*, in speaking of the neophytes who are about to share in their first communion, says: "Before saying 'This is the Lamb of God,' the celebrant may briefly remind the neophytes of the pre-eminence of the eucharist, which is the climax of their initiation and the center of the whole Christian life" (243).

It seems appropriate that this directive might be adapted for the first communion liturgy. If Eucharist is "the climax" of initiation, the candidates might be "presented" or "called" in the same fashion in which they are "called" in the confirmation liturgy before the bishop's homily. In this case, the catechist might call the name of each candidate. As the candidate's name is announced, he or she would step into the center aisle. Once all are "present," the presider, lifting the bread and wine, would make a short, declarative statement about the pre-eminence of the Eucharist. For example, he might say: "Look at this bread. This is the bread of new life. Look at this cup. This is the cup of salvation. This is the Lamb of God, who takes away the sins of the world ...."

The communion song would begin as soon as the people have responded, "Lord, I am not worthy ...." As soon as the communion song begins, the candidates process directly to the altar. They receive the bread from the presider and the cup from one of the communion ministers. After all the candidates have shared communion, the rest of the assembly processes for communion as usual.

If the communion ministers in your parish usually share communion before the assembly, on this occasion they might receive after so that the communion candidates may proceed directly to the altar table.

The musicians have to figure out a smooth way of beginning the communion song. The music should begin immediately after the "Lord, I am not worthy..." statement by the assembly. There should be no announcement of page numbers and song titles.

That means the assembly will have to know beforehand what song is to be sung. The question is, when to announce it? There is no ideal time. If your parish uses hymnals than have ribbons attached, the announcement could be made at the beginning of the liturgy, and everyone could mark the song with a ribbon. If you parish uses hymn boards, the members of the assembly could simply look there for the reference. A printed worship aid might also solve the problem. Most ideal, but perhaps most difficult, is to choose a song everyone knows by heart.

Some songs that work well for the procession during communion include:

◆ "Song of the Body of Christ," David Haas

◆ "I Am the Bread of Life," Suzanne Toolan, SM

◆ "One Bread, One Body," John Foley, SJ

◆ "Gift of Finest Wheat," Robert Kreutz and Omer Westendorf

◆ "Taste and See," James Moore

Role of the Assembly

The role of the assembly is to share communion with one another and, in doing so, to become the Body of Christ. There has been no change in theology about this, but there has been a change in the way we use our imaginations. Since the Second Vatican Council, the church has taught more clearly that we become one not only with Christ, but also with each other in the action of communion. So, whereas in a previous era, we might imagined that we were to use this time to focus on Christ *within* us, we now understand that we are to focus on Christ *around* us. Or, another way to say it is we are to focus on Christ *within the assembly*.

Role of the First Communion Candidates

The role of the candidates is to participate fully for the first time at the Lord's banquet table. In this action, they become full members of the Body of Christ. Communion is the culmination of the initiation they began at baptism.

Preparation

Pastoral planning team

Everything the catechist had done up to this point is to prepare for this moment—the first communion of the candidates. If the catechist has done the job well, the candidates will know that this is not a private encounter with Jesus, but a public, communal uniting with the Body of Christ. The catechist will need to help the candidates understand that they are not only taking

Jesus into themselves, they are becoming one with their brothers and sisters in the Lord.

The catechist and the rest of the team will want to determine exactly how the sharing of communion will happen and rehearse the action ahead of time.

Parish

The parish prepares for this moment by celebrating every communion as a sign of unity with all the members of the Body of Christ. It will take a shift in understanding for many parishioners to expand their thinking about this moment beyond a personal experience of grace. Many of us were taught to spend some quiet time with the Lord after receiving communion. While it is important to spend quiet time with the Lord, communion is not the time to do it. The purpose of communion is to become one with Christ not *only* through sharing in the consecrated bread and wine, but also in seeing Christ in our brothers and sisters around us. The parish will best prepare themselves and the first communicants for this moment by making a regular Sunday practice of participating actively in communion. Specifically, that means parishioners participate in the communion ritual every Sunday by sharing the bread and cup, by singing the communion song, by singing the song of praise after communion, and by praying in their hearts as the presider prays the prayer after communion.

The parish can also model good participation for the candidates by remaining on their feet throughout the entire communion ritual—both before and after they share communion. This is the posture called for in the *General Instruction of the Roman Missal* (21), and it is a more active posture than sitting or kneeling.

First communion families

Families can prepare by sharing meals at home. At least once a week, the whole family might gather for a well-planned meal. It need not be elaborate, but it might include an uncut loaf of bread and perhaps even wine. If not wine, some special drink. However, first communion should not be the first time children taste wine. Most do not like the taste at first because it is new to them. It will help them to have tasted wine before, perhaps at Thanksgiving, Christmas, and Easter celebrations in the home.

First communion candidates

In addition to preparing along with their families, the candidates will want to practice the communion ritual. They will need to learn how to approach the altar, how to hold their hands, how to make eye contact, when to say "Amen," how to accept the bread and the cup, and how to return to their places in the assembly.

Song after Communion

Purpose

The purpose of the song after communion is for the Body of Christ—the gathered assembly—to give praise to God.

Planning Comments

The primary consideration for the song after communion is that it be one of praise. It is also important to remember this is not to be a song of eucharistic adoration. Musicians will want to plan a song that the assembly knows and sings well.

Although it often happens, it is not appropriate to plan a communion meditation song. The action of communion is one of unity for service. It is the climax of the liturgy. At this point in the liturgy, the appropriate ritual action is for us to sing out our praise to God for having made us one. If the assembly is put in a passive role immediately after sharing communion, the rite is diminished and the meaning is obscured.

According to the GIRM, the assembly stands to sing the post-communion song.

Some good songs to sing after communion include:

◆ "I Come with Joy to Greet the Lord"

◆ "Let All Things Now Living"

◆ "Now Thank We All Our God"

◆ "Glory and Praise to Our God," Dan Schutte

◆ "Anthem," Tom Conry

◆ "Bring Forth the Kingdom," Marty Haugen

Role of the Assembly

The role of the assembly is to sing praise to God with the enthusiasm that is engendered by sure faith.

Role of the First Communion Candidates

The role of the candidates is to follow the model of the assembly, thanking God with their song.

Preparation

Pastoral planning team

The catechist prepares for this moment by having provided the candidates with ample opportunities to learn the song of praise that will be used so they may participate fully.

The rest of the team prepares for this point in the liturgy by seeing to it that the assembly has an adequate repertoire of songs of praise that they feel comfortable singing.

Parish

The parish has no particular preparation for this moment beyond singing and learning the post-communion songs during the regular Sundays of the church year.

First communion families

Families can prepare for this moment by getting a copy of the song that will be sung after communion and helping the candidates to learn it. They can also spend one of their meal times talking and sharing faith about the text of the song.

First communion candidates

The candidates might be involved in helping to pick the post-communion song to be used at the first communion liturgy. The musician or the catechist could give the candidates a few possible songs to choose from. They sing through them as a group. They might also share faith over the texts either with each other or with their families. Then, as a group, they could pick the one that seemed to fit best for them.

Prayer after Communion

Purpose

The purpose of the prayer after communion is not thanksgiving. That is the nature of the eucharistic prayer. The prayer after communion is one that asks that the gift of the eucharist will be spiritually effective in us and in the world.

Planning Comments

In some parishes, the announcements are made before the prayer after communion. This happens because of an incorrect understanding of the structure of the liturgy. The communion rite is not over until the prayer after communion is completed. The announcements, if there are any, take place during the closing rites.

As with the rest of the communion rite, the proper posture for this prayer is standing.

Role of the Assembly

The role of the assembly is to focus on the prayer, praying along with the presider.

Role of the First Communion Candidates

Like the assembly, the role of the candidates is to silently join themselves in the prayer as the presider proclaims it.

Preparation

Pastoral planning team

The catechist prepares for this moment by praying over the text ahead of time. The prayer can serve as a guide to the catechist for the entire preparation process.

The presider prepares for this point in the ritual by rehearsing the prayer after communion out loud several times.

Parish

The parish has no particular preparation to make for this moment in the rite.

First communion families

First communion families can prepare for this part of the rite by getting a copy of the prayer after communion and praying it after the family meals during the week before first communion.

First communion candidates

The candidates can prepare for this moment by praying the prayer with their families after meals.

Understanding the Preparation of Gifts

The preparation of gifts is a transition moment in the liturgy. It is often the case that transition moments become overburdened with "extras" in an attempt to add to the specialness or solemnity of the liturgy. This is, in fact, what happened to this part of the liturgy during the middle ages.

The early Christians simply and informally placed the eucharistic elements on the altar at this point in the liturgy. This was parallel to Christ taking the bread and cup at the Last Supper. There was no more to it than pointing out that these would be the elements to be used. In the middle ages, however, this simple ritual gradually expanded. The altar was dressed, gifts were "processed" to the altar and incensed, prayers were said over the gifts, and, eventually, private prayers to be said by the priest were added. Some of these prayers became quite complex and began to anticipate what was prayed for in the eucharistic prayer. Some of them began to "offer" the bread and wine to the Father in the manner of sacrifice— duplicating the meaning of the eucharistic prayer. The rite came to be called the "offertory" because of these offering prayers.

With Vatican II, the reformers simplified this rite, renaming it and removing the offering language from the prayers over the gifts. Even though the rite is simplified, it is still much more elaborate than the early

Christians would have been comfortable with. Yet, we are sometimes tempted by the same tendencies as our ancestors in the middle ages. We want to add other gifts to be brought up, add more commentary and more music, make the dressing of the altar much more elaborate, and so on. Unfortunately, these actions do little to enhance the deeper meaning and purpose of this rite, and they run the danger of detracting from the much more important moment for which the rite is intended to "prepare"—the eucharistic prayer.

The primary idea to keep in mind is that this rite is supposed to be an action of the assembly, presenting the eucharistic elements—the gifts of the community—for offering in the eucharistic prayer. It is also suitable that the assembly bring forward money for the maintenance of the community mission and gifts for the poor. But these are the only elements to be brought forward. Other gifts that have some significance to a special group within the assembly may have some meaning to that group, but they do not have a meaning or place in this ritual.

The members of the assembly would ordinarily present these gifts to the priest or deacon at the altar—not at the foot of the sanctuary. The music that accompanies the rite would ordinarily be paced to end when the rite ends.

Faith-Sharing Questions for Eucharistic Prayer III

Father, you are holy indeed,
and all creation rightly gives you praise.

- What is holiness?
- What does it mean to be holy?

All life, all holiness comes from you
through your Son, Jesus Christ, our Lord,
by the working of the Holy Spirit.
From age to age you gather a people
  to yourself,
so that from east to west
a perfect offering may be made

- What is the perfect offering?
- Why does God need to gather people so the offering can be made?
- What is the purpose of the offering?

to the glory of your name.
And so, Father, we bring you these gifts.
We ask you to make them holy by the power
  of your Spirit,

- What did you say holiness was above?
- How does it apply to these gifts?
- How does the Spirit make them holy?

so that they may become the body +
  and blood
of your Son, our Lord Jesus Christ,

- What do we mean by "body and blood?"
- Do we really believe the bread and wine become body and blood?

at whose command we celebrate
  this eucharist.
On the night he was betrayed,
he took bread and gave you thanks and praise.

- What is Jesus giving thanks and praise for?
- What do we give thanks and praise for in this prayer?

He broke the bread, gave it to his disciples,
  and said:

- Do you break bread or cut it?
- Why did Jesus break it?

Take this, all of you, and eat it:
this is my body which will be given up
  for you.

- Why did Jesus use *bread* to identify his body?

When supper was ended, he took the cup.
Again he gave you thanks and praise,

- What is Jesus giving thanks and praise for?
- What do we give thanks and praise for in this prayer?

gave the cup to his disciples, and said:
Take this, all of you, and drink from it:

- Based on this prayer, what is the more important symbol: the wine or the action of drinking from the cup? Why?

this is the cup of my blood,
the blood of the new and everlasting covenant.

- If this is the cup of the new covenant, what was the old covenant?

It will be shed for you and for all
so that sins may be forgiven.
Do this in memory of me.

◆ What is it we are to do to remember
Jesus? How does this action help us
remember him?

Let us proclaim the mystery of faith:

◆ What is the "mystery" of our faith?

1. Christ has died,
Christ is risen,
Christ will come again.

2. Dying you destroyed our death,
rising you restored our life.
Lord Jesus, come in glory.

3. When we eat this bread and drink
   this cup,
we proclaim your death, Lord Jesus,
until you come in glory.

4. Lord, by your cross and resurrection
you have set us free.
You are the Savior of the world.

◆ Read each of these options aloud. Do they
all mean the same thing?
◆ Which one most clearly expresses your
own faith?
◆ Which least expresses your faith?
◆ Can you think of another way to say
what the mystery of faith is?

Father, calling to mind the death your Son
   endured for our salvation,
his glorious resurrection and ascension
   into heaven,
and ready to greet him when he comes again,

◆ Is this true? Are we ready to greet Jesus
when he comes again?
◆ What would that look like?

we offer you in thanksgiving this holy
   and living sacrifice.

◆ What sacrifice are we offering?
◆ In what way is it holy?
◆ In what way is it living?

Look with favor upon your Church's offering,
and see the Victim whose death has reconciled
   us to yourself.

◆ Rephrase this sentence in your own
words and discuss what it means to you.

Grant that we, who are nourished by his
   body and blood,
may be filled with his Holy Spirit,

◆ Do you believe the body and blood of
Christ fill you with the Holy Spirit?
◆ How and when does that happen?
◆ What happens to you when that happens?

and become one body, one spirit in Christ.

◆ What does it mean to become "one body,
one spirit in Christ"?

May he make us an everlasting gift to you
and enable us to share in the inheritance
   of your saints,
with Mary, the virgin Mother of God;
with the apostles, the martyrs,
(Saint N.—the saint of the day
   or the patron saint)

◆ What "saint" would you add here if you
could?

and all your saints,
on whose constant intercession we rely
   for help.

◆ How does the intercession of the saints
help us?

◆ Why are we calling for their intercession in this prayer?

> Lord, may this sacrifice,
> which has made our peace with you,
> advance the peace and salvation
>   of all the world.

◆ How exactly does "this sacrifice" advance the peace and salvation of the world?
◆ Do you have anything to do with it, or is all up to God?

> Strengthen in faith and love
>   your pilgrim Church on earth;
> your servant, Pope N., our bishop N.,

◆ Do you know who the pope is?
◆ Do you know who your bishop is?
◆ Why do they show up in this prayer?

> and all the bishops,
> with the clergy and the entire people
>   your Son has gained for you.
> Father, hear the prayers of the family
>   you have gathered here before you.
> In mercy and love unite all your children
>   wherever they may be.
> Welcome into your kingdom
>   our departed brothers and sisters,
> and all who have left this world
>   in your friendship.

◆ Who do you pray for during this part of the prayer?
◆ Why do we pray for our departed loved ones in this prayer?

> We hope to enjoy forever the vision
>   of your glory,

◆ What do you think the vision of God's glory looks like?

> through Christ our Lord,
>   from whom all good things come.
> Through him,
> with him,
> in him,
> in the unity of the Holy Spirit,
> all glory and honor is yours,
> almighty Father,
> for ever and ever.

◆ Read this last sentence aloud. This sentence ends every version of the eucharistic prayer. Why do you think that is?
◆ What does this sentence mean?

> (Amen.)

◆ This "amen" is always supposed to be sung. Why do you think that is?
◆ How would you summarize the main point of this prayer?

Wheat-and-Water Only Bread Recipe

Adapted from "Bread Recipe: Wheat-and-Water Only Bread," *The Triduum Book*, by The Editors of MODERN LITURGY, © 1997 Resource Publications, Inc. All rights reserved.

Makes five or six 18-piece loaves.

2½ cups whole wheat flour
1¼ cups warm water
½ cup unbleached white flour
1½ tsp. salt (optional)

(Metric equivalents: 1 cup = 235 ml, 1 tsp = 5 ml)

Preheat oven to 350°F (180°C). Gather bowls, tools, and ingredients. Measure and mix dry ingredients. Sift twice. Measure hot tap water into small mixing bowl. Add liquids. Mix—dough will be sticky. If dry, add ⅛ cup (60 ml) warm water. Stir. If necessary, add ⅛ cup more water and stir. Dust counter with flour. Knead dough 5–6 minutes. When dough is smooth, form a ball, cover it with a dampened cloth, and let it rest 5 minutes. Coat cookie sheet with oil.

Variation *(small scored rounds)*
Separate dough into three baseball-size balls of dough. Take one ball, smooth it and sprinkle lightly with flour. Roll out ⅜–½ inch (1.0–1.2 cm) thick and 4½ inches (11.5 cm) round. Stamp out a 4½-inch (11.5 cm) circle. Save scraps. Deeply imprint a 2½-inch (6.5 cm) circle in the center. Score vertically through center. Score inner circle horizontally. Score deeply six sections on each side of vertical score. Transfer loaf to cookie sheet with spatula. Use scraps to make some 2½-inch (6.5 cm) loaves. Stamp with circle and imprint cross on each. Start preparing the next batch.

Bake at 350°F (180°C) for 10 minutes. Remove from oven. Lightly brush loaves with oil. Return to oven. Bake 10 minutes more. Remove from oven. Sample for taste and chewiness. If too chewy, bake 3–5 minutes more. Transfer loaves to paper-towel-covered plates. Blot 3–5 minutes.

Original Recipe *(large, unscored rounds)*
Separate dough into two equal balls. Roll each ball out ¼ inch (0.6 cm) thick and 8 inches (20 cm) across. Place each round onto cookie sheet. If baking more than one batch, start preparing the next batch as soon as first batch is in oven. Bake at 350°F (180°C) for 16-17 minutes. Remove from oven. Sample taste and chewiness. If too chewy, bake 3–5 minutes more. Transfer loaves to paper-towel-covered plates. Blot 3–5 minutes. If using immediately, place loaves on a platter. Cover loosely for transport. If storing, cool loaves. Wrap each loaf loosely in microwave wrap. Place in a plastic container. Refrigerate or freeze.

PART FOUR

Concluding Rites

Concluding Rites

Overview

In the concluding rites, we receive God's blessing and then go out into the world to live the life we have just practiced in the Eucharist. That is, we go out to practice Christ-like love for one another.

The concluding rites are also the time for any announcements that need to be made.

Outline of the Rites

Bracketed text indicates optional rite.

- [Announcements]
- Greeting
- Blessing
- Dismissal
- [Recessional Song]

Catechist Background Sheets

- Examples of Prayers over the People (from the sacramentary)
- Guidelines for Writing Announcements

Recommended Reading

Johnson, Lawrence J. "Concluding Rites." *The Word and Eucharist Handbook*. Rev. ed. San Jose: Resource Publications, Inc., 1993. 134 ff.

"Concluding Rite." *The Mystery of Faith*. Washington, DC: Federation of Diocesan Liturgical Commissions, 1981. 125–134.

Wagner, Nick. "How should we handle the announcements after Mass?" *Modern Liturgy Answers the 101 Most-Asked Questions about Liturgy*. San Jose: Resource Publications, Inc., 1996. 52 ff.

Jorgensen, Susan S. "The Dismissal Rite: A Blessing for Action." *Modern Liturgy* 19 (Oct. 1992): 18–21.

The concluding rite consists of:
a. the priest's greeting and blessing, which on certain days and occasions is expanded and expressed in the prayer over the people or another more solemn formulary;
b. the dismissal of the assembly, which sends each member back to doing good works, while together praising and blessing the Lord (GIRM 57).

The concluding rite consists of the priest's greeting and blessing, which is sometimes expanded by the prayer over the people or another solemn form, and the dismissal which sends forth each member of the congregation to do good works, praising and blessing the Lord (GI, No. 57) (MCW 49)

The comments that precede the final blessing (see IG 11) are important in Masses with children. Before they are dismissed they need some repetition and application of what they have heard, but this should be done in a very few words. In particular, this is the appropriate time to express the connection between the liturgy and life (DMC 54).

Any necessary announcements are to be kept completely separate from the homily; they must take place following the prayer after communion (LMln 27).

Announcements

Purpose

The purpose of the announcements is to conduct business of the community that cannot be done in another, more effective way.

Planning Comments

The placement of the announcements has varied over the centuries. In the early middle ages in Rome, the deacon made the announcements right after the pope received communion but before anyone else did. That is probably because most of the assembly was no longer sharing communion, and many of them left during communion.

Another earlier practice was to join the announcements to the end of the homily. That, too, happened in many parishes until very recently. In some communities, there is still a temptation to do this for some announcements.

The best place for the announcements, for the sake of the liturgy, is where the *General Instruction of the Roman Missal* places them—immediately before the greeting and final blessing (123).

Announcements are optional, and most announcements can be eliminated with no damage done to either the liturgy or the event that was to be announced. However, at a first communion liturgy, there may be information that must be shared for the good of the community. For example, if there is a parish reception immediately following, it is hospitable to let people know that. It might also be appropriate for the presider to lead the assembly in a round of congratulatory applause for the first communicants during the announcements.

There is a temptation to use the announcements as a time to thank all those who helped plan the liturgy. This presents a theological and ritual problem. The Eucharist is not a production for which the cast and crew are called out to take their bows. The liturgy is first and foremost the work of the people. It is the assembly that does the "work" and the assembly that should take the credit.

If the planners are to be thanked, a more meaningful way would be in the manner recommended by old fashioned etiquette—handwritten thank-you notes following the event. By thanking the planners in this way, the liturgy is not disrupted, there is little chance of forgetting to thank someone, and the thanks is more genuine in that it takes some planning and personal sacrifice.

Liturgy planners will want to take great care, especially for the first communion liturgy, to see that the closing rites do not become over-burdened with activity. The climax of the liturgy is communion. The concluding rites are *anticlimactic* and should be done as smoothly and simply as possible.

Role of the Assembly

The primary liturgical reform of the Second Vatican Council was to call for the full, conscious, and active participation of the assembly. The announcements cause a danger of putting the assembly into a passive role. To minimize that danger, keep these guidelines in mind. First, the announcements need to be general enough to be of interest to most members of the assembly. Next, the announcements need to be short. When you think they are short enough, shorten them again. Be sure the assembly is standing when the announcements are made. Standing is a more active position than sitting. If the announcements are too long for the assembly to comfortably stand through, they are much too long.

Finally, the only things that really need to be announced are those events that are happening when you walk out the door. Everything else can go in the bulletin.

Role of the First Communion Candidates

The role of the candidates is to follow the example of the rest of the assembly and to participate as they do.

Preparation

Pastoral planning team

The catechist might want to check to see that the announcements for the first communion liturgy are not too long so they don't distract from the liturgy. The catechist might even take charge of writing the announcements for this liturgy.

If not the catechist, then someone on the pastoral planning team needs to be responsible for writing and editing the announcements based on the guidelines above. The team also needs to be sure that the person making the announcements rehearses them beforehand.

Parish

The parish as a whole has no particular preparation to make for the announcements, but they participate in them by listening attentively.

First communion families and first communion candidates

The families and candidates have no particular preparation to make for the announcements.

At least sometimes, depending on the liturgical seasons and different occasions in the children's life, the priest should use more expanded forms of blessing, but at the end should always retain the Trinitarian formulary with the sign of the cross (DMC 54).

In a word, God bestows his blessing by communicating or declaring his own goodness; his ministers bless God by praising him and thanking him and by offering him their reverent worship and service. Whoever blesses others in God's name invokes the divine help upon individuals or upon an assembled people (*Book of Blessings* 6).

Greeting and Final Blessing

Purpose

The next element of the concluding rites, the blessing, is the most important. A blessing is a powerful thing that we perhaps take too lightly at times. A blessing given by God is always a promise of divine help and a sign of God's favor.

Planning Comments

The sacramentary offers three options for the blessing. Form A, the "simple form," is the one we most often hear at Mass on Sundays. Occasionally, especially during the more solemn liturgical seasons, the presider might use Form B, the "solemn blessing." The first communion celebration would be an appropriate time to use one of the solemn blessings.

The third option, Form C, is seldom used. This "prayer over the people" offers twenty-six different blessings. It takes a little hunting to find them in the sacramentary, but if you can find the main final blessing page, there will be a note under Form C telling you where to find the twenty-six texts. In the 1974 edition of the sacramentary published by the Catholic Book Publishing Co., they begin on page 581.

Role of the Assembly

The role of the assembly is to pay close attention to what is asked for in the blessing and to join themselves with the presider in asking for God's blessing. When the solemn blessing is used, the assembly responds with a three-fold amen. The solemn blessings are usually not written in a way that makes it obvious when the assembly is to respond, so it will require an extra measure of attention on their part.

Role of the First Communion Candidates

The role of the candidates is to follow the example of the rest of the assembly and to participate as they do.

Preparation

Pastoral planning team

The catechist can prepare by becoming more familiar with the way blessings work and by using blessings throughout the preparation process. The introduction to the *Book of Blessings* offers a concise yet thorough theology of blessings along with practical suggestions. Some of the twenty-six blessings in the sacramentary, identified as Prayers over the People, can be used not only for the first communion liturgy but also as conclusions to each of your preparation sessions before sending the children home. There are also many blessings in the *Book of Blessings* that can be used during the preparation sessions. These include the Order for the Blessing of Baptized Children, the Order for the Blessing of Students and Teachers, the Order of Blessing on the Occasion of a Birthday, and many others.

The catechist might suggest which blessing to use for the liturgy or at least suggest a few options to select from. In addition, the catechist can use the blessing that will be used at the liturgy as part of the dismissal from the preparation sessions.

The greeting and blessing will be more effective if the presider practices them out loud beforehand. They can be sung or chanted as a way of adding solemnity to the celebration.

Parish

With the help of the pastoral team, the parish as a whole can prepare for better participation in the final blessing by celebrating full, liturgical blessings at other times of the year. Many Catholics are used to getting things blessed—things like pets, cars, houses, rosaries, etc. The *Book of Blessings* reminds us that, "Blessings are a part of the liturgy of the church" (16). As such, a blessing requires all the elements of good liturgy, most importantly "the participation of at least some of the faithful" (17). In other words, however simple, blessings should always be celebrations of a gathered assembly. By settling for a simple wave of the hand or sprinkling of holy water by the priest, parishioners are risking "the intrusion into the celebration of ... that [which] might replace genuine faith with superstition and/or shallow credulity" (19).

First communion families

First communion families can prepare for fuller celebration of the final blessing by regularly practicing blessings in the home. A modified version of the *Book of Blessings* is available for home use. It is titled *Catholic Household Blessing and Prayers*, and it contains many blessings that can be easily celebrated in the home throughout the liturgical year.

First communion candidates

The candidates can prepare by celebrating blessings with the parish and with their families throughout their preparation process. In addition, the candidates can make a regular practice of asking God's blessing on their loved ones. This might be particularly appropriate during their night prayers.

Dismissal

Purpose

After the blessing comes the dismissal. The action, however, is more like a commissioning to joyfully go forth into the world to live out the Gospel (GIRM 57).

Planning Comments

Originally, there was no dismissal nor even a blessing in the Mass. Very soon, however, worshipers felt some need for a formal sending out. The word "Mass" comes from the Latin word for dismissal—*missa*.

It is the deacon's job to dismiss the assembly. In his absence, the presider does the dismissal. There are three options for the dismissal, all of which emphasize the peace of Christ. The assembly responds by saying, "Thanks be to God." As with the blessing, the dismissal and the response might be sung on solemn occasions.

As with the greeting at the beginning of Mass, the dismissal is more effective if it is not "supplemented" with an informal statement such as, "Have a nice day." Off the cuff remarks like this trivialize the profound meaning of sending the assembly out to live in the peace of the Lord.

The final element of the closing rites is the exiting of the ministers. The first communicants might also join in the closing procession, but it would be appropriate only if they did so with their families.

No closing song is listed in GIRM. It is a common element of most Masses, but it is not required. If a song of praise is sung after communion, the recessional might be accompanied by a strong organ piece or other instrumental music. Some suggestions include:

◆ "Prelude in F Major," J.S. Bach

◆ "Prelude in G Major," J.S. Bach

◆ "Toccata in F Major," Dietrich Buxtehude

◆ "Canticle of the Sun," Marty Haugen

Role of the Assembly

The role of the assembly is to remain actively engaged in the liturgy at this point. There can be a temptation to slip into the role of spectators, particularly if the announcements are long or the ritual drags.

[T]he dismissal of the assembly ... sends each member back to doing good works, while praising and blessing the Lord (GIRM 57b).

Role of the First Communion Candidates

The role of the candidates is to enjoy the moment. They have spent much time preparing for this event, and now it is about to end. They will want to try to remember as much as they can about this day because it has the potential to be one of the more formative moments in their lives.

Preparation

Pastoral planning team

The catechist and the pastoral team will want to do some planning about where photos might be taken after the liturgy. If the families will want to take photos of their children with the pastor in the sanctuary, it might be best to have the pastor and the children remain in their places during the recessional. In that case, only the cross and the lectionary would make up the closing procession.

Another option is to arrange for photos to be taken before Mass. This gets everyone to church in time for the liturgy keeps the after-Mass activities from becoming confusing.

Parish

The parish might prepare a reception immediately following the first communion. Many of the families will have probably planned parties at their homes, so the reception should be a very simple affair.

First communion families

Traditionally, families give their children a gift after the children share in their first communion. Some common gifts include a Bible, a rosary, or a cross. Some other possible gifts include an icon, a book of prayers, or storybook. When considering a gift, don't get something only because it seems "holy." Give a gift that will actually be used and appreciated.

First communion candidates

Younger candidates can prepare for the post-communion activities by trying to be on their best behavior. Younger children especially may be worn out by this time and there is still much to do in the day. It may be difficult for children to get beyond the pressures of being in the center of attention for such an extended period of time. However, to the extent they are able, they will have taken one more step on their journey as loving, faithful disciples.

A recessional song is optional. The greeting, blessing, dismissal, and recessional song or instrumental music ideally form one continuous action which may culminate in the priest's personal greetings and conversations at the church door (MCW 49).

Examples of Prayers over the People (from the sacramentary)

Lord,
grant your people your protection and grace.
Give them health of mind and body,
perfect love for one another,
and make them always faithful to you.
Grant this through Christ our Lord.
(Amen.)

Lord,
send your light upon your family.
May they continue to enjoy your favor
and devote themselves to doing good.
We ask this through Christ our Lord.
(Amen.)

Lord,
we pray for your people who believe in you.
May they enjoy the gift of your love,
share it with others,
and spread it everywhere.
We ask this in the name of Jesus the Lord.
(Amen.)

Lord,
help your people to seek you
   with all their hearts
and to deserve what you promise.
Grant this through Christ our Lord.
(Amen.)

Lord,
grant that your faithful people
may continually desire to relive the mystery
   of the Eucharist
and so be reborn to lead a new life.
We ask this through Christ our Lord.
(Amen.)

Lord God,
in your great mercy,
enrich your people with your grace
and strengthen them by your blessing
so that they may praise you always.
Grant this through Christ our Lord.
(Amen.)

May God bless you with every good gift
   from on high.
May he keep you pure and holy in his sight
   at all times.
May he bestow the riches of his grace
   upon you,
bring you the good news of salvation,
and always fill you with love for all men.
We ask this through Christ our Lord.
(Amen.)

Lord,
come, live in your people
and strengthen them by your grace.
Help them to remain close to you in prayer
and give them a true love for one another.
Grant this through Christ our Lord.
(Amen.)

Guidelines for Writing Announcements

1. Limit the number of announcements. If you have to make more than three, the assembly grows restless and will probably not remember most of what is announced.

2. Limit the length of the announcements. Try to keep announcements under three sentences.

3. Only announce things that cannot be taken care of in the bulletin. If there is a breakfast immediately after Mass, it needs to be announced. Parishioners will not go home, read the announcement in the bulletin, and then come back to church. But if the breakfast is next Sunday, it does not need to be announced.

4. Do not reward lateness. By scheduling announcements that did not get into the bulletin by deadline day, you are encouraging people to be late in the future.

5. Do not announce dates, times, places, or phone numbers. Simply announce the event or cause and refer the assembly to the bulletin for details. For example, "If you have yet not begun the first communion preparation process, see the bulletin for details on how to get started."

6. Do not make announcements during the homily time.

7. Avoid passive sentence constructions. Passive: "Parishioners are needed to help with the first communion preparation process." Active: "We need your help to prepare our children for first communion."

APPENDICES

A: How to Use This Book to Supplement Your First Communion Program

If you are using one of the first communion preparation programs listed in Appendix A, look up the week or the session in the program and then turn to the appropriate part of *Meaningful First Communion Liturgies* for supplementary background information. *Meaningful First Communion Liturgies* is not designed to replace your first communion preparation program, but it can help make the link between the preparation program and the first communion liturgy itself.

B: Resources

The resources in Appendix B are designed to help parishes and families have a more meaningful experience of first communion. Use them as they are written or adapt them for the particular needs of your community.

C: First Communion Liturgy Planning Sheets

Appendix C consists of three planning sheets. The first is for the Third Sunday of Easter and can be used in any cycle. I have included several suggestions and ideas, but you can adapt them as needed for your community. If you celebrate first communion on another Sunday in Easter, you can still use many of the ideas here. The second planning sheet is for a celebration of first communion outside the Easter season. The readings come from the Votive Mass for Holy Eucharist. Again, adapt as necessary. The third planning sheet is a blank template. Photocopy this and use it to plan your own liturgies from the ground up.

The Table of the Lord (Ave Maria)

Page citations in bulleted text refer to pages in *Meaningful First Communion Liturgies* (MFCL). Other page citations refer to the first communion preparation program under discussion unless preceded by "MFCL."

Group Session 1 — "We Celebrate"
◆ Read "Overview" of the Opening Rites, page 9.
◆ Connect with "Gathering," page 10.
◆ Connect with "Opening Song," page 12.
◆ Connect with "Sign of the Cross, Greeting, Introduction," page 16.
◆ Connect with "Final Blessing," page 86.

Consider modeling the gathering for your session on the gathering as you would like it to happen on Sundays. Have greeters available. Provide a welcoming atmosphere. Be sure everyone knows where to go. Remember that many of the families may not know each other, so have someone on hand who is good at making introductions and starting conversations.

Instead of immediately splitting the children off from their parents, consider gathering everyone together first to sing an opening song. This can model the purpose and action of the opening song on Sunday. Be sure it is one that everyone knows. After the song, the children can be sent to their own area.

If you do the prayer at the end of the children's session on page 33, be sure to begin and end with the sign of the cross to get the children in the habit of making this gesture every time they pray. You might also consider using one of the twenty-six options for the "Prayer over the People" in the sacramentary as an alternative to the prayer given in the director's book. You can also use one of these twenty-six prayers as a conclusion to the "We Celebrate" prayer service (pages 33–37). The sacramentary prayers are not always written in child-friendly language and may need some adapting, but the images and thoughts expressed in them reflect the tradition of the church.

Group Session 2 — "We Show We Care"
◆ Connect with "Lord's Prayer and Sign of Peace," page 60.
◆ Connect with "Profession of Faith and Prayer of the Faithful," page 38.

As an alternative to having the children hold hands for the Lord's Prayer at the end of their session (page 41), consider having them pray with their hands in the "orans" position. This is the gesture the assembly will use during the Lord's Prayer after the revised sacramentary is approved.

Also, you can suggest to the families and the children that they pray the Lord's Prayer three times each day — morning, noon, and evening. This was the ancient practice of Christian households during the first few centuries of the church.

The Table of the Lord (Ave Maria) (continued)

Group Session 3
◆ Connect with "Preparation of Altar and Gifts," page 52.
◆ Read "Overview" of the Communion Rite, page 59.
◆ Connect with "Fraction Rite," page 64.
◆ Connect with "Communion" page 68.

As a way of connecting Eucharist and the home meal, encourage families to plan one meal a week that is a special, family meal. Ideally, this would take place on Sunday. That meal should always include bread that is broken, not cut, and perhaps even a glass of wine for the adults. The children might receive a ritual taste. Or they might have grape juice of their own.

Session 1 — Celebrating
◆ Read "Overview" of the Opening Rites, page 9.
◆ Connect with "Gathering," page 10.
◆ Connect with "Opening Song," page 12.
◆ Connect with "Sign of the Cross, Greeting, Introduction," page 16.

Be sure to begin and end all preparation sessions with the sign of the cross. Encourage families to always make the sign of the cross when they pray at home.

Session 2 — Forgiving
◆ Connect with "Penitential Rite and Sprinkling Rite," page 17.

You can supplement the material by explaining that we sometimes celebrate a sprinkling rite instead of a penitential rite at Mass to remind us of our baptism. If you are using the *Family Book*, you might provide an alternate litany for the one on

page 34. The invocations there are focused on the sin of the individual. If you compare it with the "Lord, have mercy" invocations in the sacramentary, you will find the sacramentary prayers to be more focused on praise and thanksgiving for having been reconciled or rescued from sin.

Session 3 — Listening
◆ Read "Overview" of the Liturgy of the Word, page 29.
◆ Connect with "First and Second Readings," page 30.
◆ Connect with "Psalm and Alleluia," page 33.
◆ Connect with "Gospel and Homily," page 35.

Session 4 — Caring
◆ Connect with "Profession of Faith and Prayer of the Faithful," page 38.

Session 5 — Giving
◆ Read "Overview" of the Liturgy of the Eucharist, page 51.
◆ Connect with "Preparation of Altar and Gifts," page 52.

Session 6 — Sharing
◆ Connect with "Eucharistic Prayer," page 55.

Session 7 — Remembering
◆ Connect with "Eucharistic Prayer," page 55.

Session 8 — Belonging
◆ Read "Overview" of the Communion Rite, page 59.
◆ Connect with "Lord's Prayer and Sign of Peace," page 60.

The Table of the Lord (Ave Maria) (continued)

Session 9 — Receiving
◆ Connect with "Fraction Rite," page 64.
◆ Connect with "Call to Communion," page 66.
◆ Connect with "Communion," page 68.

Try not to over-emphasize the aspect of "receiving" in this session to the point that the children think of themselves as passive recipients. It is true that we do "receive" the gift of Christ's Body and Blood. But in that moment, we are the Body of Christ, and at the same time we are receiving, we are also offering (cf. *Catechism of the Catholic Church* 1368; 1 Cor 10:16–17). "Sharing" is a word that might be used in place of "receiving" when speaking of communion.

Session 10 — Serving
◆ Read "Overview" of the Concluding Rites, page 83.
◆ Connect with "Greeting and Final Blessing," page 86.
◆ Connect with "Dismissal," page 88.

We Celebrate the Eucharist (Silver Burdett and Ginn)

Page citations in bulleted text refer to pages in *Meaningful First Communion Liturgies*.

Theme 1 —
The Eucharist Is About Belonging

◆ Read "Overview" of the Opening Rites, page 9.
◆ Read "Overview" of the Communion Rite, page 59.
◆ Connect with "Gathering," page 10.
◆ Connect with "Penitential Rite and Sprinkling Rite," page 17.
◆ Connect with "Communion," page 68.

Theme 2 —
The Eucharist Is About Celebrating

◆ Read "Overview" of the Opening Rites, page 9.
◆ Connect with "Gathering," page 10.
◆ Connect with "Opening Song," page 12.
◆ Connect with "Sign of the Cross, Greeting, Introduction," page 16.

Theme 3 —
The Eucharist Is About Listening

◆ Read "Overview" of the Liturgy of the Word, page 29.
◆ Connect with "First and Second Readings," page 30.
◆ Connect with "Psalm and Alleluia," page 33.
◆ Connect with "Gospel and Homily," page 35.

Theme 4 —
The Eucharist Is About Caring

◆ Connect with "Profession of Faith and Prayer of the Faithful," page 38.

Theme 5 —
The Eucharist Is About Making Peace

◆ Read "Overview" of the Communion Rite, page 59.
◆ Connect with "Penitential Rite and Sprinkling Rite," page 17.
◆ Connect with "Lord's Prayer and Sign of Peace," page 60.

Theme 6 — The Eucharist Is About Giving Thanks for Creation

◆ Read "Overview" of the Liturgy of the Eucharist, page 51.
◆ Connect with "Preparation of Altar and Gifts," page 52.
◆ Connect with "Eucharistic Prayer," page 55.

Theme 7 — The Eucharist Is About Giving Thanks for New Life

◆ Connect with "Eucharistic Prayer," page 55.

Theme 8 — The Eucharist Is About Sharing a Meal

◆ Connect with "Fraction Rite," page 64.
◆ Connect with "Call to Communion," page 66.
◆ Connect with "Communion," page 68.

Theme 9 — The Eucharist Is About Going Forth to Make a Better World

◆ Read "Overview" of the Concluding Rites, page 83.
◆ Connect with "Greeting and Final Blessing," page 86.
◆ Connect with "Dismissal," page 88.

Celebrating the Gift of Jesus (Brown-Roa)

Page citations in bulleted text refer to pages in *Meaningful First Communion Liturgies* (MFCL). Other page citations refer to the first communion preparation program under discussion unless preceded by "MFCL."

Lesson 1 — We Belong to God's Family

- Read "Overview" of the Opening Rites, page 9.
- Connect with "Gathering," page 10.
- Connect with "Opening Song," page 12.
- Connect with "Sign of the Cross, Greeting, Introduction," page 16.
- Connect with "Penitential Rite and Sprinkling Rite," page 17.

Instead of doing the dramatization of a baptism suggested in the teacher's manual, consider taking the children to a regularly scheduled parish baptism. It may be more work, but it will also be more effective. If you do opt for the dramatization, be sure that you, as a catechist, worship at a parish baptism beforehand so your dramatization will be accurate. Consider doing the dramatization in the church, with all the elements that would ordinarily be used in a baptism. Also consider immersing the doll into the font instead of pouring water over its head. Immersion is the preferred method of baptism.

Consider rephrasing the question on page 29 in the teacher's manual, "What do we say to show that we want God's forgiveness." The answer given, "Lord have mercy," is not quite accurate. "Lord, have mercy" is a statement of praise that can and is used at times that are not penitential. When it is used in the penitential rite at Mass, it is a statement of praise to Christ because he saved us from sin and death.

Lesson 2 — We Listen to God's Word

- Read "Overview" of the Liturgy of the Word, page 29.
- Connect with "First and Second Readings," page 30.
- Connect with "Psalm and Alleluia," page 33.
- Connect with "Gospel and Homily," page 33.
- Connect with "Profession of Faith and Prayer of the Faithful," page 38.

Lesson 3 — Gifts of Bread and Wine

- Read "Overview" of the Liturgy of the Eucharist, page 51.
- Connect with "Preparation of Altar and Gifts," page 52.

Avoid the suggestion at paragraph 17 on page 42 in the teacher's manual that the children prepare a special gift box to present during the preparation of gifts during the first communion liturgy. Additional gifts detract from the primary gifts, which are the bread and wine. Also, to imply that the children give of themselves in a special way by offering a gift other than the bread and wine implies that their gifts of bread and wine are not special and are not fully representative of themselves. This is the wrong message to send at first communion time. If you want to make the presentation more concrete for the children, consider having some of them help bake the bread that will be offered in the Eucharist. Have some others go shopping with you or with their parents to buy the wine that will be offered.

Celebrating the Gift of Jesus (Brown-Roa) (continued)

Lesson 4 — Jesus Shares Himself
◆ Connect with "Eucharistic Prayer," page 55.

Lesson 5 — We Receive Jesus
◆ Read "Overview" of the Communion Rite, page 59.
◆ Connect with "Lord's Prayer and Sign of Peace," page 60.

Lesson 6 — We Thank God for Jesus
◆ Connect with "Fraction Rite," page 64.
◆ Connect with "Call to Communion," page 66.
◆ Connect with "Communion," page 68.

Lesson 7 — We Celebrate Eucharist
◆ Connect with "Opening Song," page 12.
◆ Connect with "Preparation of Altar and Gifts," page 52.
◆ Connect with "Eucharistic Prayer," page 55.
◆ Connect with "Communion," page 68.

You might want to deal with the dismissal rite, which is not covered extensively in this program. It would be important for the children to understand that communion is an action that leads to service in the world.

Adult Session: Belonging
◆ Read "Overview" of the Opening Rites, page 9.
◆ Connect with "Gathering," page 10.
◆ Connect with "Opening Song," page 12.
◆ Connect with "Sign of the Cross, Greeting, Introduction," page 16.

Adult Session: Sharing the Body of Christ
◆ Read the "Overview" of the Communion Rite, page 59.
◆ Connect with "Fraction Rite," page 64.
◆ Connect with "Call to Communion," page 66.
◆ Connect with "Communion," page 68.

Adult Session: Thanksgiving Celebration
◆ Read "Overview" of the Liturgy of the Eucharist, page 51.
◆ Connect with "Eucharistic Prayer," page 55.

First Eucharist (Benziger)

Page citations in bulleted text refer to pages in *Meaningful First Communion Liturgies* (MFCL). Other page citations refer to the first communion preparation program under discussion unless preceded by "MFCL."

Lesson 1 — We Gather
◆ Read "Overview" of the Opening Rites, page 9.
◆ Connect with "Gathering," page 10.
◆ Connect with "Opening Song," page 12.
◆ Connect with "Sign of the Cross, Greeting, Introduction," page 16.

Lesson 2 — We Are Sorry
◆ Connect with "Penitential Rite and Sprinkling Rite," page 17.

You can supplement the material by explaining that we sometimes celebrate a sprinkling rite instead of a penitential rite at Mass to remind us of our baptism. If you are using the *Family Edition*, you might provide an alternate litany for the one on page 15. The invocations there are focused on the sin of the individual. If you compare it with the "Lord, have mercy" invocations in the sacramentary, you will find the sacramentary prayers to be more focused on praise and thanksgiving for having been reconciled or rescued from sin.

Lesson 3 — We Listen Jesus
◆ Read "Overview" of the Liturgy of the Word, page 29.
◆ Connect with "First and Second Readings," page 30.

◆ Connect with "Psalm and Alleluia," page 33.
◆ Connect with "Gospel and Homily," page 35.
◆ Connect with "Profession of Faith and Prayer of the Faithful," page 38.

Lesson 4 — We Bring the Gifts
◆ Read "Overview" of the Liturgy of the Eucharist, page 51.
◆ Connect with "Preparation of Altar and Gifts," page 52.

Lesson 5 — We Remember
◆ Connect with "Eucharistic Prayer," page 55.

Lesson 6 — We Pray
◆ Read "Overview" of the Communion Rite, page 59.
◆ Connect with "Lord's Prayer and Sign of Peace," page 60.

Lesson 7 — We Share Jesus
◆ Connect with "Fraction Rite," page 64.
◆ Connect with "Call to Communion," page 66.
◆ Connect with "Communion," page 68.

Lesson 8 — We Help Others
◆ Read "Overview" of the Concluding Rites, page 83.
◆ Connect with "Greeting and Final Blessing," page 86.
◆ Connect with "Dismissal," page 88.

Around the Lord's Table
(Our Sunday Visitor)

Page citations in bulleted text refer to pages in *Meaningful First Communion Liturgies* (MFCL). Other page citations refer to the first communion preparation program under discussion unless preceded by "MFCL."

Lesson 1 — Jesus Is the Light Of God's Family
◆ Read "Overview" of the Opening Rites, page 9.
◆ Connect with "Penitential Rite and Sprinkling Rite," page 17.

Lesson 2 — We Have a Parish Family
◆ Connect with "Gathering," page 10.
◆ Connect with "Opening Song," page 12.
◆ Connect with "Sign of the Cross, Greeting, Introduction," page 16.

Lesson 3 — We Ask Forgiveness
◆ Connect with "Penitential Rite and Sprinkling Rite," page 17.

You can supplement the material by explaining that we sometimes celebrate a sprinkling rite instead of a penitential rite at Mass to remind us of our baptism. If you are using the *Teacher Guide*, you want to be careful of the introduction to the word "mercy" on page 34. It asks the leader to have the children guess the meaning of "mercy" and gives the correct answer as "forgiveness." A dictionary would more likely define "mercy" as "compassion." "Compassion" means to "with (com) feeling (passion)." To say Christ feels what we feel is different than saying Christ forgives us.

"Compassion" may be beyond the children's vocabulary, but it doesn't help to give them an incorrect definition.

A secondary definition, and one truer to the original liturgical use of the word "mercy," is "blessing." To ask Christ to "have mercy" is to both bless Christ and to ask for Christ's blessing. If you read the "Lord, have mercy" invocations in the sacramentary, you will find the sacramentary prayers to be more focused on praise and thanksgiving for Christ's "blessings" of reconciliation and salvation.

Lesson 4 — We Listen to God's Word
◆ Read "Overview" of the Liturgy of the Word, page 29.
◆ Connect with "First and Second Readings," page 30.
◆ Connect with "Psalm and Alleluia," page 33.
◆ Connect with "Gospel and Homily," page 35.
◆ Connect with "Profession of Faith and Prayer of the Faithful," page 38.

Lesson 5 — We Prepare Our Gifts
◆ Read "Overview" of the Liturgy of the Eucharist, page 51.
◆ Connect with "Preparation of Altar and Gifts," page 52.

Lesson 6 — We Welcome Jesus, The Bread of Life
◆ Connect with "Eucharistic Prayer," page 55.

Around the Lord's Table (Our Sunday Visitor) (continued)

Lesson 7 — At the Lord's Table

◆ Read "Overview" of the Communion Rite, page 59.

◆ Connect with "Lord's Prayer and Sign of Peace," page 60.

◆ Connect with "Fraction Rite," page 64.

◆ Connect with "Call to Communion," page 66.

◆ Connect with "Communion," page 68.

Lesson 8 — We Do the Work of Jesus

◆ Read "Overview" of the Concluding Rites, page 83.

◆ Connect with "Greeting and Final Blessing," page 86.

◆ Connect with "Dismissal," page 88.

First Eucharist (Sadlier)

Page citations in bulleted text refer to pages in *Meaningful First Communion Liturgies* (MFCL). Other page citations refer to the first communion preparation program under discussion unless preceded by "MFCL."

Session 1 — "We Gather Together"
◆ Read "Overview" of the Opening Rites, page 9.
◆ Connect with "Gathering," page 10.
◆ Connect with "Penitential Rite and Sprinkling Rite," page 17.
◆ Connect with "Gloria," page 19.
◆ Connect with "Opening Song," page 12.
◆ Connect with "Sign of the Cross, Greeting, Introduction," page 16.

The program suggests a "Parish Welcoming Rite" (page G9 in the leader's guide and page 4 in the participant's book). The program suggests placing the rite immediately before the final blessing. Consider adapting the rite to make it more of a blessing of the candidates and less a statement of commitment on the part of the candidates. For example, the rite, as presented, concludes with a kind of profession of faith. That might be adapted so that the presider invites the community to lay hands on the candidates and pray for God's blessing on them so their faith will be strengthened.

For Session 1, the leader's guide suggests placing the participant's guide inside the Bible when reading the Scripture passage for the session (page G11). The possible confusion of symbols that this may cause could easily be avoided by simply reading the selected text directly from the Bible itself. If the catechist finds the adapted text that is presented in the participant's guide

more helpful than the actual Scripture, he or she might try using the Contemporary English Version Bible (American Bible Society). This is the translation that is used in the Lectionary for Masses with Children.

Session 2 — We Listen
◆ Read "Overview" of the Liturgy of the Word, page 29.
◆ Connect with "First and Second Readings," page 30.
◆ Connect with "Psalm and Alleluia," page 33.
◆ Connect with "Gospel and Homily," page 35.
◆ Connect with "Profession of Faith and Prayer of the Faithful," page 38.

Session 3 — We Give Gifts
◆ Read "Overview" of the Liturgy of the Eucharist, page 51.
◆ Connect with "Preparation of Altar and Gifts," page 52.

Session 4 — We Remember
◆ Connect with "Eucharistic Prayer," page 55.

The leader's guide makes the point that the catechist, when speaking with the children, should keep in mind the basic structure of the eucharistic action: 1) taking, 2) blessing, 3) breaking (or pouring, for the cup), 4) eating, and drinking (page G16). It is primarily through this four-part action that we remember Jesus. Later the guide suggests asking the children, "What happens at the consecration of the Mass?" The question seems to locate all the emphasis of the four-part action on the consecration. Most theologians today speak of the entire eucharistic prayer as being

First Eucharist (Sadlier) (continued)

consecratory. It might be better to ask the children how Jesus becomes present in the Mass. Christ becomes present in several ways, as the *Constitution on the Sacred Liturgy* makes clear; these include being present in the ministers of the liturgy, in the sacred word, and in the gathered assembly (CSL 7). Christ is present especially under the eucharistic elements. In the four-part structure of the eucharistic action, it is the offering of the eucharistic prayer by the priest united with the assembly that blesses or consecrates those elements. While this is too much information to communicate to the candidates, the catechist must understand how Christ is present in the liturgy. The goal is to avoid focusing on one isolated moment within a very rich and complex rite.

The leader's guide also suggests bringing forward the children's notes to Jesus in the preparation of gifts procession. It is best to avoid including any elements other than the bread, wine, and collection in the preparation of gifts (see MFCL 52).

Session 5 — We Receive Jesus

◆ Read "Overview" of the Communion Rite, page 59.
◆ Connect with "Lord's Prayer and Sign of Peace," page 60.
◆ Connect with "Fraction Rite," page 64.
◆ Connect with "Call to Communion," page 66.
◆ Connect with "Communion," page 68.

Try not to overemphasize the aspect of "receiving" in this session to the point that the children think of themselves as passive recipients. It is true that we do "receive" the gift of Christ's Body and Blood. But in that moment, we are the Body of Christ and at the same time we are receiving, we are also

offering (cf. *Catechism of the Catholic Church* 1368; 1 Cor 10:16–17).

In the four-part structure of action of the Eucharist (leader's guide, page G16), the fourth action is "eating and drinking" which has a more active connotation that "receiving." The leader's guide does point out that up until this point in the liturgy we have done most of what Jesus asked us to do in remembrance of him. The final action is "sharing" (page G18). "Sharing" is a word that might be used in place of "receiving" when speaking of communion.

It will also be important to *consistently* speak of sharing both the living *bread* and the saving *cup*. It might be helpful to adapt "My Communion Prayer" on page 44 of the participant's guide to include both bread and cup.

The leader's guide stresses that it is important to help children understand they may share the living bread either by taking it in their hands or having it placed on their tongues. While this is true, it is difficult to understand why the more passive "receiving on the tongue" would enjoy equal emphasis with sharing food in a more active and usual manner.

The "After Receiving Communion" section on page 47 in the participant's guide suggests that the first communicants "spend time just with Jesus." This seems inconsistent with the understanding that Jesus is present in the midst of the gathered assembly and that sharing communion unites us not only with Jesus, but with the our brothers and sisters in Christ. We all become one body and cannot at that moment detach ourselves from the body to be "just" with Jesus.

First Eucharist (Sadlier) (continued)

Session 6 — Jesus Is with Us Always

◆ Read "Overview" of the Concluding Rites, page 83.

◆ Connect with "Sign of the Cross, Greeting, Introduction," page 16.

◆ Connect with "Greeting and Final Blessing," page 86.

◆ Connect with "Dismissal," page 88.

Tips for Families

Take your child to Mass every week.
Your child's formation for first communion is based primarily on the celebration of the liturgy. If you miss Mass, the formation will be weak. Each Mass is important, but more important is the discipline of weekly prayer and worship with the community. Many times people think getting to Mass two or three times a month is enough. However, a child formed in this way quickly learns that faith is a matter of convenience.

Arrive on time.
Sometimes it can be difficult to get to Mass on time, especially if you have more than one child. But make an extra effort, especially during the formation period for first communion. The liturgy is like a story and to get the full effect of the story you need to be there from the beginning. You may feel like you are not missing much, but your child may be understanding some of the songs and rituals and readings for the first time during this preparation period. Don't shortchange your child by arriving late.

Sit up front.
This is especially important if your church is arranged in such a way that it is difficult for your child to see. In order to participate in and understand the Mass, your child needs to be able to see what's going on.

Pray and sing with the assembly.
You need to be a strong role model for your child. If you do not participate fully, neither will your child. Parents are the first teachers of faith. By your example, you pass on the tradition of our faith to your children.

Share communion every week.
Most Catholics partake of communion every week. For a very few, there may be a good reason why they cannot. However, sometimes people refrain from communion unnecessarily. If you are not sharing in communion every week, please speak with your pastor about it. The strongest way you can show your child that communion is important is by sharing in communion yourself.

Discuss the readings with your child before Mass.
Many times the readings for the coming week are printed in the Sunday bulletin. There are also many resources available that print the weekly readings. Preparing ahead of time will have a big impact on your child's ability to understand the readings. Even reading just the Gospel out loud a day or two before Mass will help.

Discuss the homily with your child after Mass.
Some preachers are better than others, but most are not speaking to children when they preach on Sunday. However, almost all preachers have a core message they are trying to communicate. You can help your child understand that message by discussing the homily each week. Ask your child to try to remember one interesting phrase each week and discuss that.

First Communion Information For Families

What to Wear for First Communion

There are no special requirements for what to wear for first communion. In some families and some ethnic groups, there is a tradition of girls wearing white dresses and boys wearing a white shirt and tie. If this is true in your case, you can still follow that guideline. White is a very appropriate color for first communion because it reminds us of the white garment all of us were clothed in at our baptism. The clothes do not need to be elaborate or expensive. Something very simple can also be very elegant.

All the parish asks is that you and the candidate "dress up" to make this day seem special. That should not have to mean purchasing any new clothes. Remember this is "first" communion, and there will be many more. It is not like a wedding that happens only once. So use your best judgment in deciding what the candidate will wear. The goal is for the candidate to remember that this day is important but not to feel awkward or conspicuous.

What the Candidate Should Carry

Nothing. Please leave all Bibles, rosaries, crosses, and anything else at home. These items will only be in the way. If you would like a devotional item blessed, please see to that before the day of the first communion liturgy.

Pictures

First communion is a very important time for you and the candidate. The most important part of the event is, of course, the prayer you will make together in the liturgy and the sharing of communion.

However, sometimes the prayer and the communion can seem secondary to a younger candidate who is asked to "pose" for pictures throughout the liturgy. Flash bulbs and video lights distract you and your child from focusing on the prayer. They distract the rest of the assembly also.

The parish prefers that no one take any pictures or videos during the liturgy. Plenty of time will be available for picture taking with the presider after Mass is over. But if you must take pictures or videos, we ask that you not use any flashes or lights. We also ask that you restrict yourselves to one still camera and one video camera per family. Your family photographers *may not* move around during the liturgy, nor may they enter the sanctuary. They also are required to sit or kneel when the rest of the assembly is doing so.

Please make copies of this notice to give to friends or members of your family whom you think might be tempted to take pictures during the liturgy. Please help the candidate and the rest of the parish make this first communion a special and prayerful event.

Thank you for your cooperation.

Sample Bulletin Announcements

When writing bulletin announcements, try to avoid using language that identifies the staff or the volunteers as a group separate from the rest of the parish. For example, do not write: "We ask you to participate ...." Instead write, "It is important for all of us to participate ...." Look at every bulletin announcement as an opportunity to catechize the parish. Do so in such a way that presumes the parishioners are as excited about the parish mission as you are. Use language that praises the good things parishioners do. You might adapt these examples for your community.

Several families have begun asking about how to prepare their children for first communion. The family is primarily responsible for forming children in the faith and bringing them to the table. However, all of us have a role to play. These families need help in catechizing their children, and they need the emotional and spiritual support of the whole parish. It would be a great service to them and to the whole parish if you could share your faith life with these young people over the several months. Call [N.] at [parish phone number] if you can give an hour a week over the next [number of] months. The schedule is flexible if you need to take some weeks off for work or vacation. If you cannot give any extra time, would you be willing to pray for one of the first communion candidates during his or her time of preparation? Please call if would like the name of someone to pray for.

In [number of] weeks, our parish will begin formally preparing children for the celebration of first communion. If you would like to prepare your child, please call [N.] at [parish phone number]. The primary place of formation will be at Mass on Sunday and in your home life. However, volunteers in the parish will help you by spending an hour a week during the next [number of] months with the children of the parish who are getting ready to join us at the table. We will also have sessions for the parents to help you with the skills and tasks you need to make sure your children will be ready to share communion with us.

This week, a number of children will begin their preparation for celebrating first communion. The focus of their preparation will be the celebration of the Sunday liturgy. All of us can help them by being strong role models for them. Most of us participate in the liturgy pretty well. It will be important for all of us to make an extra effort to participate in the liturgy these next few months for the sake of the children. The children learn from our example—from our singing and praying—what is important about our faith. It will be especially important for all of us to provide an example by sharing in communion each week. If there is something that prevents anyone from sharing in communion, please contact Fr. [N.] at [parish phone number] to see what can be done to make it possible for you to join us at the table.

Sample Bulletin Announcements (continued)

Next Sunday, a number of children will be joining us at the Lord's Table for the first time at the [time of] Mass. As a parish, we will want to keep them and their families in our prayers. These young people have been preparing for many months, primarily by coming here to worship every Sunday and following our example. They are grateful for the models in faith that everyone in the parish has been for them. Please continue to support them by coming next Sunday and participating as fully as possible in the liturgy. If there is anyone who is unable to share in communion with these young people because of some impediment, please call Fr. [N.] at [parish phone number] to see what can be done to make if possible for you to join us at the table.

First Communion Liturgy Planning Checklist

One Year Out
- ❏ Send announcements about the process.
- ❏ Put the first communion celebration on the parish calendar.
- ❏ Order books if you will be using a textbook.
- ❏ Plan and schedule all bulletin announcements.
- ❏ Reserve meeting space for all the preparation sessions.

Six Months Out
- ❏ Determine what readings will be used for the liturgy if the celebration is not on a Sunday. Or look up the readings that will be used if it is on a Sunday. (Catechists and parents can refer to these readings throughout the preparation.)
- ❏ Determine what prayers will be used in the Mass if the celebration is not on a Sunday. Or look up the prayers that will be used if it is on a Sunday. (Catechists and parents can refer to these prayers throughout the preparation.)

Three Months Out
- ❏ Determine what music will be used in the liturgy. If need be, teach new music to the candidates during the preparation process.
- ❏ Complete a first draft of the liturgy outline using the template on page 120. Circulate to other members of the pastoral planning team.
- ❏ Check with the person who schedules liturgical ministers to be sure you will have dependable help available.

- ❏ Schedule a rehearsal of the liturgy.
- ❏ Make a rough layout of a worship aid if you will be using one. Contact at least three printers if don't have one you already use. Ask about deadlines and prices.

One Month Out
- ❏ Circulate a final draft of the liturgy outline.
- ❏ Discuss homily ideas with the pastoral team and the homilist.
- ❏ Send camera-ready worship aid to the printer.
- ❏ Find a volunteer to bake bread for the liturgy.
- ❏ Be sure enough wine is on hand for communion from the cup.

One to Two Weeks Out
- ❏ Pick up worship aid from the printer.
- ❏ Make pew cards identifying where families will sit.
- ❏ Do the rehearsal.
- ❏ Check with the maintenance staff to be sure the church will be clean for the celebration. If there is no staff, schedule volunteers for cleaning.

The Day Before
- ❏ Place pew cards on the pews.
- ❏ Place worship aids in the pews (or give to the ushers to hand out the next day).
- ❏ Check for any clutter in the entryways or the sanctuary.

On the Day
- ❏ Set out communion cups if necessary.

3rd Sunday of Easter

- Cycle A: Acts 2:14:22–28; 1 Pt 1:17-21; Lk 24:13–35
- Cycle B: Acts 3:13–15,17–19; 1 Jn 2:1–5; Lk 24:35–38
- Cycle C: Acts 5:27–32,40–41; Rv 5:11–14; Jn 21:1–19

Focus of the Readings
The disciples recognize and remember Jesus in the sharing of a meal.

Environment and Art Notes
This is the Easter season, so the environment that is already in place should be sufficient. Sometimes there is a temptation to add to the environment for this one day. This is usually unnecessary and can even be distracting because the space winds up being "too much." If the Easter lilies are fading they may need to be replaced. If a special font was constructed for Easter, the water may need to be replenished. But that should be all that is required.

Ritual Notes
Again, since this is the Easter season, the ritual will likely be quite "full" already. Be careful not to overburden it. Ideally, the sprinkling rite takes the place of the penitential rite every Sunday of Easter and it would do so on this day. You might be sure to use incense in the opening procession and to bless the gifts, but this should also happen on all the other Sundays of Easter. One addition you might make to the liturgy is to have the first communion candidates process into church during the opening song. However, some members of their families should accompany them to symbolize the role of the family in the preparation of the candidates.

Prelude
- Ps 122: "Let Us Go Rejoicing," musical setting by J. Michael Joncas

Children other than the first communion candidates can join the choir to do this psalm. Some children can play Orff instruments on the bass notes of each chord and others use the triangle and maybe a recorder or two.

Gathering Song
- "Glory to God" from Alexander Peloquin's *Mass of the Bells* (GIA)

Refrain only with instrumental interludes; some children—other than the first communion candidates—can accompany with handbells.)

Order of Procession
- Cross Bearer
- [Incense Bearer]
- Candle Bearers
- [First Communion Candidates and Their Families]
- Lectors
- Deacon with the Book of the Gospels (If your parish has no deacon, one of the lectors carries the Book of the Gospels or the lectionary.)
- Presider

3rd Sunday of Easter (continued)

Sign of the Cross and Greeting: Option A

The music continues softly underneath.

The best choice for the greeting might be Option A in the sacramentary. After the greeting, "the priest, deacon, or other suitable minister may very briefly introduce the Mass of the day." The best option might be no introduction at all. This will already be a "full" liturgy, and adding more words to it may do more harm than good. If an introduction is necessary, it might be appropriate for the coordinator of the first communion program, the director of religious education, or the school principal to make this introduction. It should be no more than one or two sentences, and it should be well rehearsed. "Rehearsed" means not only knowing the lines well but also knowing exactly when to deliver them so there is no lag in the liturgy. The introduction might read: "In today's Gospel, the disciples recognize the risen Christ when he shares a meal with them. Today, we, too, will recognize Christ as we share the heavenly banquet with several candidates for first communion at our table."

Sprinkling Rite: Option C

If the blessing is prayed, the music continues underneath; otherwise, the singing of the Gloria resumes as soon as the ministers begin sprinkling the assembly. This time, sing the entire Gloria, except for the Amen.

Ideally, you will use water from the baptismal font, which was blessed at the Easter Vigil. If that is the case, the presider can skip the blessing of water that precedes the sprinkling. If the water needs to be blessed, Option C is to be used during the Easter season.

The presider does not need to be the only minister sprinkling the assembly. Liturgical dancers, members of the choir, or other members of the assembly can assist.

Gloria

The singing of the Gloria—except for the Amen—takes place during the sprinkling. Music continues underneath the opening prayer.

Opening Prayer

◆ Alternative Opening Prayer for the 3rd Sunday of Easter

Sing the Amen from the Gloria as the conclusion to the opening prayer.

Either the first opening prayer or the alternative is appropriate. The first prayer speaks of restoring the "joy of our youth," however, and that may sound odd to the first communion candidates.

First Reading

Reader:

It is not appropriate for the first communion candidates to serve as lectors. The lectors for this liturgy should be the best the parish has to offer.

The proclaimer should, through the style of proclamation, answer the question, "What is the most important phrase in this reading?"

Psalm Response

◆ Ps 118: "This Is the Day the Lord Has Made," J.M. Joncas.
◆ Richard Proulx also has a setting in which the refrain can be done in round with the assembly.

The psalm is always sung.

3rd Sunday of Easter (continued)

Second Reading
Reader:

The proclaimer should, through the style of proclamation, answer the question, "What is the most important phrase in this reading?"

Gospel Acclamation
◆ "Alleluia" from *Mass of the Bells*, Alexander Peloquin (GIA)

The Gospel acclamation is always sung. It is not necessary to include the verse with the alleluia, but if you do, it is also to be sung. If the Gospel acclamation is not sung, it is omitted. The solemnity of the Easter season and the first communion liturgy make a Gospel procession appropriate. However, if you have a small worship space, a Gospel procession might be "too much" for the space.

Gospel
Reader:

The proclaimer should, through the style of proclamation, answer the question, "What is the most important phrase in this reading?" The solemnity of the occasion makes it appropriate for the Gospel to be sung, but only if the proclaimer is an excellent singer. Even a poor singer, however, could at least intone "The Gospel of the Lord" at the end of the reading. The people would intone the response, "Praise to you Lord, Jesus Christ."

Homily (Key Points to Make)
In each of the Gospels for all three cycles, Jesus is eating. In Cycle A, the Emmaus story, the purpose of these meals is most clear, but it is the same in all the readings. At his last meal before he died, Jesus told the disciples to remember him primarily through meal-sharing or "bread-breaking." When Jesus appears to the disciples after the resurrection, he eats with them so they will recognize him, so they will "remember" him. The key point to make for the first communion liturgy is that the communicants will also recognize or "remember" Jesus in the meal they are about to share.

Profession of Faith (Nicene Creed, Apostles' Creed, or Baptismal Promises)
The profession of faith could be done in question-and-answer fashion as is done in the renewal of baptismal promises during the Easter Vigil.

Prayer of the Faithful
Include at least one prayer for each of the following:

◆ the church
◆ the world
◆ the oppressed
◆ the local community
◆ the first communion candidates
◆ those who have died

Will this be sung or spoken?
Who will sing or read?

It is not appropriate to have the first communion candidates read the petitions. (See Role of the First Communion Candidates, "Profession of Faith and Prayer of the Faithful," page 38.) The solemnity of the season makes it appropriate that the cantor sing the intercessions. Or a member of the assembly—even one of the parents of the first communicants—might read the petitions.

3rd Sunday of Easter (continued)

Preparation of Altar and Gifts
◆ "Seed Scattered and Sown," Dan Feiten (Text: Didache 9, the earliest form of the eucharistic prayer). Assembly on refrain, choir on verses.

Gift bearers:

It is not appropriate for first communion candidates to be gift bearers. (See Role of the First Communion Candidates, "Preparation of Altar and Gifts," page 52.) Some of their friends or family members might serve in this role, however.

Will the gifts be incensed?

Preface:
Eucharistic Prayer for Children I
Will this be sung or spoken?

The solemnity of this liturgy makes the singing of the preface appropriate if the presider is even a passable singer. The preface for Easter II is perhaps the most appropriate.

Eucharistic Prayer:
Eucharistic Prayer for Children I

Holy, Memorial Acclamation, Great Amen
◆ Acclamations from *Mass of Creation*, M. Haugen, or *Mass of the Bells*, Alexander Peloquin

Use the same setting throughout the Easter season. The acclamations of the eucharistic prayer are always sung.

Lord's Prayer

Lamb of God
◆ *Mass of Creation* or *Mass of the Bells*

Ideally, everyone remains standing during the entire communion rite. This is the direction given in the *General Instruction of the Roman Missal* (21). If you decide to follow this practice in your parish, you would want to do it at least every Sunday of the Easter season, if not every Sunday of the year. The communion rite begins with the Lord's Prayer and ends with the prayer after communion.

Song during Communion
◆ Ps 34: "Taste and See," M. Haugen

Song of Praise and Thanksgiving after Communion
◆ "Bring Forth the Kingdom," M. Haugen, or "I Am the Bread of Life," S. Toolan

Everyone remains standing for this song. It is not appropriate to have the choir or a soloist do a "meditation" song at this point in the liturgy.

Blessing
Will the blessing be sung?

Recessional Music
A sung recessional is optional; if the assembly does not sing, the organist can play Widor's "Tocatta," or the choir/folk ensemble can sing an upbeat hymn or song.

Order of Recession
◆ Cross Bearer
◆ Other Servers
◆ [First Communion Candidates and Their Families]
◆ Lectors
◆ Deacon with the Book of the Gospels
◆ Presider

Votive Mass for Holy Eucharist (When First Communion Is Not Celebrated on a Sunday)

◆ 1 Kgs 19:4–8; Ps 116; 1 Cor 10:16–17; Lk 24:13–35

Focus of the Readings

God comes to us in the form of a meal. We recognize Christ, we are strengthened, and we become one.

Environment and Art Notes

Try to respect the environment that is already in place. If it is ordinary time, however, you may want to add some flowers and festive banners to the decor. The best solution is to enlist the help of the regular environment committee. They know what is available and what works best in your worship space. Be sure not to surround the altar with flowers or anything else. Even if the candidates will not be coming directly to the altar, it needs to appear to be approachable. Banks of flowers create an unnecessary barrier. Don't forget to also decorate the assembly space. The assembly is the primary minister in the liturgy.

Ritual Notes

The sprinkling rite would ordinarily take the place of the penitential rite at the first communion liturgy. You can make the liturgy more festive by using incense at one or all of the points of the Mass where it is called for. These are the opening rites, the Gospel procession, and the preparation of gifts. Another addition you might make to the liturgy is to have the first communion candidates process into church during the opening song. However, some members of their families should accompany them to symbolize the role of the family in the preparation of the candidates.

Prelude

Children other than the first communion candidates can join the choir to do this psalm. Some children can play Orff instruments on the bass notes of each chord and others use the triangle and maybe a recorder or two.

Gathering Song

Order of Procession

◆ Cross Bearer
◆ [Incense Bearer]
◆ Candle Bearers
◆ [First Communion Candidates and Their Families]
◆ Lectors
◆ Deacon with the Book of the Gospels (If your parish has no deacon, one of the lectors carries the Book of the Gospels or the lectionary.)
◆ Presider

Sign of the Cross and Greeting: Option A

After everyone is in place, they freeze for a moment. The music from the opening song ends. Then, without much delay, the music that will accompany the sprinkling rite begins softly. The presider then begins the greeting.

Votive Mass for Holy Eucharist (continued)

Sprinkling Rite: Option B

As the presider prays the blessing over the water, the music for the Gloria begins to gradually build. As he concludes with "Grant this through Christ our Lord," the music comes up full and the assembly begins to sing. The sprinkling of the assembly also begins. The presider does not need to be the only minister sprinkling the assembly. Liturgical dancers, members of the choir, or other members of the assembly can assist.

Song during the Sprinkling

Opening Prayer

◆ From the Votive Mass of the Holy Eucharist, Option A

The music from the sprinkling rite continues softly underneath the prayer.

First Reading

◆ 1 Kgs 19:4–8

Reader:

It is not appropriate for the first communion candidates to serve as lectors. The lectors for this liturgy should be the best the parish has to offer.

The proclaimer should, through the style of proclamation, answer the question, "What is the most important phrase in this reading?"

Psalm Response

◆ Ps 116

The psalm is always sung.

Second Reading

◆ 1 Cor 10:16–17

Reader:

The proclaimer should, through the style of proclamation, answer the question, "What is the most important phrase in this reading?"

Gospel Acclamation:

The Gospel acclamation is always sung. It is not necessary to include the verse with the alleluia, but if you do, it is also to be sung. If the Gospel acclamation is not sung, it is omitted. The solemnity of the first communion liturgy make a Gospel procession appropriate. However, if you have a small worship space, a Gospel procession might be "too much" for the space.

Gospel

◆ Lk 24:13–35

Reader:

The reader should, through the style of proclamation, answer the question, "What is the most important phrase in this reading?"

Homily

Profession of Faith (Nicene Creed, Apostles' Creed, or Baptismal Promises)

The profession of faith is not required on days other than Sundays and solemnities. However, it may done in solemn local celebrations. If you decided to include it, you might want to do it in question-and-answer format as is done at the Easter Vigil.

Votive Mass for Holy Eucharist (continued)

Prayer of the Faithful

Include at least one prayer for each of the following:

♦ the church
♦ the world
♦ the oppressed
♦ the local community
♦ the first communicants
♦ those who have died

Will this be sung or spoken?
Who will sing or read?

It is not appropriate to have the first communion candidates read the petitions. The solemnity of the season makes it appropriate that the cantor sing the intercessions. Or a member of the assembly—even one of the parents of the first communicants—might read the petitions.

Preparation of Altar and Gifts

Gift bearers:

It is not appropriate for first communion candidates to be gift bearers. Some of their friends or family members might serve in this role, however.

Will the gifts be incensed?

Preface: Holy Eucharist II (P 48)

Will this be sung or spoken?

The solemnity of this liturgy makes the singing of the preface appropriate if the presider is even a passable singer.

Eucharistic Prayer:
Eucharistic Prayer for Children I, II or III

Holy, Memorial Acclamation, Great Amen

You could choose a setting just for this liturgy, or you could use the one currently being used on Sundays in your parish. In either case, it should be a setting that is well known. The acclamations of the eucharistic prayer are always sung.

Lord's Prayer

Lamb of God

Ideally, everyone remains standing during the entire communion rite. This is the direction given in the *General Instruction of the Roman Missal*. If you decide to follow this practice your assembly, you would want to do it at least every Sunday of the Easter season, if not every Sunday of the year. The communion rite begins with the Lord's Prayer and ends with the prayer after communion.

Song during Communion

Song of Praise and Thanksgiving after Communion

Everyone remains standing for this song. It is not appropriate to have the choir or a soloist do a "meditation" song at this point in the liturgy.

Blessing: Prayer over the People #20

Will the blessing be sung?

Recessional Music

Order of Recession
♦ Cross Bearer
♦ Other Servers
♦ [First Communion Candidates and Their Families]
♦ Lectors
♦ Deacon with the Book of the Gospels
♦ Presider

First Communion Liturgy Planning Template

Focus of the Readings

Environment and Art Notes

Ritual Notes

Prelude

Gathering Song

Order of Procession

Greeting

Sprinkling Rite or Penitential Rite

Gloria

Opening Prayer

First Reading
Reader:

Psalm Response

Second Reading
Reader:

Gospel Acclamation

Will there be a Gospel procession?

Gospel
Reader:

Will the Gospel be sung?

Homily (Key Points to Make)

**Profession of Faith
(Nicene Creed, Apostles' Creed,
or Baptismal Promises)**

Prayer of the Faithful
Include at least one prayer for each of the
following:

◆ the church
◆ the world
◆ the oppressed
◆ the local community
◆ the first communion candidates
◆ those who have died

Will this be sung or spoken?
Who will sing or read?

Preparation of Altar and Gifts
Gift bearers:

Will the gifts be incensed?

Preface Dialogue

Will this be sung or spoken?

First Communion Liturgy Planning Template (continued)

Preface and Eucharistic Prayer

Song of Praise and Thanksgiving after Communion

Holy, Memorial Acclamation, Great Amen

Blessing

Will the blessing be sung?

Lord's Prayer

Recessional Music

Lamb of God

A sung recessional is optional.

Order of Recession

Song during Communion

EUCHARIST
An Eight-Session Ritual-Catechesis Experience for Adults

Susan S. Jorgensen

Paper, 200 pages, 8½" x 11", ISBN: 0-89390-293-4

People have noticed the power in the catechumenal process and they have wondered what comes next? Or what can be done, in a similar vein, for those who have grown up Catholic? The answer lies in continuing liturgical experience. *Eucharist*, by Susan S. Jorgensen, will help you get started. Participants in this eight-week program work through the prayers of the Eucharistic liturgy, from opening rite to dismissal, and emerge with deep understanding of the words and gestures of the Eucharist. This could be the mystagogia experience you've been looking for, or the way to help your liturgical ministers understand the heart and soul of the liturgy.

CHILDREN'S CATECHUMENATE:
A Catechist's Guide

Philip J. McBrien

Paper, 104 pages, 8½" x 11", ISBN: 0-89390-413-9

Lead your child catechumens to faith with this resourceful guide. It includes background information on the catechumenate in general, the children's catechumenate in particular, and explanation of current practice on children's catechumenate. Also includes a set of reproducible handouts for family catechesis on each period or rite and guidelines for doing periodic interviews with the families.

MODERN LITURGY ANSWERS THE 101 MOST-ASKED QUESTIONS ABOUT LITURGY

Nick Wagner

Paper, 144 pages, 5½" x 8½", ISBN: 0-89390-369-8

Everyone has a question about liturgy. Get answers from the editor of MODERN LITURGY magazine. You'll learn the historical and theological background of current liturgical practices and you'll get practical solutions to vexing pastoral problems. Use this important reference book for your planning or just to provide quick authoritative answers.

CATECHIZING WITH LITURGICAL SYMBOLS
25 Hands-on Sessions for Teens and Adults

Pamela J. Edwards

Paper, 128 pages, 8½" x 11", ISBN: 0-89390-401-5

These 25 liturgical symbols will touch you. You know the power of symbols. The power to inspire. To enrich. To deepen faith. But most resources on symbols are dry, wordy, theoretical treatises. Not this one. *Catechizing with Liturgical Symbols* is a practical, 25-session program for expanding family understanding and sensitivity for symbols. In these sessions, people interact with these symbols, are touched by them, and let them become a part of their faith experience. Creating symbols can also be used as therapeutic exercises that promote healing. The examples included in this work can be done at home, in the classroom or with a worship environment, all with a minimum of aesthetic training and only a small investment in time or money.

Order from your local bookseller, or contact:

 Resource Publications, Inc.
160 E. Virginia Street #290
San Jose, CA 95112-5876
1-408-286-8505 (questions)
1-408-287-8748 (fax)
1-888-273-7782 (orders, toll-free)
info@rpinet.com
www.rpinet.com